# Is This Working?

## The Businesslady's Guide to Getting What You Want from Your Career

☑ Navigating a Job Search

☑ Managing Your Time

☑ Dealing with Coworkers

☑ Making Your Job Work for You

## COURTNEY C.W. GUERRA
A.K.A. the Businesslady

Adams Media
New York   London   Toronto   Sydney   New Delhi

*For Doug.*
*Anytime. Dinner? Literally any time.*

Adams Media
An Imprint of Simon & Schuster, Inc.
57 Littlefield Street
Avon, Massachusetts 02322

First Adams Media trade paperback edition APRIL 2017

ADAMS MEDIA and colophon are trademarks of Simon and Schuster.

For information about special discounts for bulk purchases, please contact Simon & Schuster Special Sales at 1-866-506-1949 or business@simonandschuster.com.

The Simon & Schuster Speakers Bureau can bring authors to your live event. For more information or to book an event contact the Simon & Schuster Speakers Bureau at 1-866-248-3049 or visit our website at www.simonspeakers.com.

Interior design by Colleen Cunningham

Manufactured in the United States of America

10 9 8 7 6 5 4 3 2 1

Library of Congress Cataloging-in-Publication Data has been applied for.

ISBN 978-1-4405-9849-4
ISBN 978-1-4405-9850-0 (ebook)

"I'm interested in things . . .
I think I'm getting good,
But I can handle criticism.
I'll show you what I know."

—They Might Be Giants, "Doctor Worm"

# Contents

# Introduction

"What do you want to be when you grow up?"

It's a pointless question, right? You probably answered it countless times in your childhood, but is there any meaningful relationship between your response and the likely trajectory of your career? Becoming a paleontologist, or a ballerina, or an astronaut, is a much different process than becoming a project manager, or an events coordinator, or a budget analyst—but I suppose the first few have more brand recognition among the elementary-school demographic. Unless you're pursuing a field with a direct apprenticeship or degree-based track, there's no clear route from "person who's just graduated" to "actual professional." And to further complicate things, each of us needs to flail around for a bit before we're able to figure out which roles suit us best.

So I don't know what you want to be when you grow up, and my guess is that you don't either. However, I feel pretty confident about how to discover the answer to that question: you muddle your way through the working world, going from bad-fit job to okay-fit job to—finally, eventually—something that just feels *right*. You might have to repeat a few cycles of bad-fit/okay-fit before you get there, but with enough determination, it will happen. I know this because *I* got there, despite having no idea what I wanted to do with my life other than "make enough money to survive."

After my own meandering journey toward some semblance of success, I ended up an editor. (Well, I'm also a writer, but if I'm being honest editing is my real passion. And yes, I know that's weird.) As an editor, I'm constantly looking at someone else's

9

words and asking myself, in essence, "Is this working?" It's not my job to tell other writers what to say, or to force them to make revisions—I'm just there to offer some perspective. "Here's what I think you're trying to do, and here's how I think you can do that more effectively."

That's basically what this book is: a style manual for your career. No matter how you feel about grammar, you know that there are rules, and that some are more flexible than others. Certain things fall under the category of personal choice, whereas others are pretty much mandatory.

The same principle applies to the professional world as well. If you're trying to figure out how you, personally, want to do things, it's helpful to know How Things Are Done (or how they could be done, or might be done). You can decide to break as many rules as you want, but that should be an informed decision—you don't want to be shocked by the consequences.

In my Dear Businesslady column (which began on *The Toast*—now dearly departed—and is currently on *The Billfold*) I give personalized advice based on individual situations. But it's always geared toward helping a wider audience. Part of the fun of reading advice columns is crinkling your brow at the decision-making on display in the original letter—or feeling a pang of recognition. Then when you read the response, you weigh it against what seems most natural to you, how you'd handle the same scenario.

In the following pages, you'll read about situations you're likely to encounter in the workplace, along with a set of strategies for getting through them. You may agree with my advice or not (somehow, despite its obvious brilliance), but as long as I've helped you think through your own professional choices, I've done my job.

Your career will evolve out of a series of decisions—moments when you ask yourself, "Is this working?" and let your instincts be your answer. Some of these decisions will feel hugely important at the time but ultimately prove irrelevant, while others will be snap judgments that set in motion major, life-changing events. You need to consider what you enjoy, what you're good at, and what you value, and then weigh that against where you want to live, what jobs are available, how much money you want to make (versus the amount of time you want to spend making it), and a zillion other practical considerations.

It's a lot, is what I'm saying.

So if you let me handle the procedural logistics and offer guidance on the complex emotional side of things, that will free you up to focus on the bigger picture. Everyone deals with some nonsense early in their career—but that's just the rough draft. All that matters is that you end up inside the story *you* want to be telling, and I'm here to help you present the most polished version of yourself.

## CHAPTER 1

## THE FIRST RUNG:

# Navigating a Job Search

THIS IS A workplace-advice book, so my first piece of advice is that you need to find a place to work. That's a pretty involved process, which is why this is the longest chapter. Feel free to pace yourself—it's not like you're going to submit an application and then find yourself in a salary negotiation five minutes later (and if you do, I'm gonna go ahead and say that's a red flag).

Job-searching is a complex roller coaster ride of emotions, including but not limited to: excitement, frustration, confusion, anxiety, relief, and embarrassment. At the end of it all, you'll end up employed—and if you're lucky, you might even like what you're doing.

This chapter offers tips on how to reach that final step, but don't worry too much about doing everything right. In the course of my own postcollege job search, I submitted at least one cover letter with a glaring typo (e.g., "Businesslday") and wasted two separate days interviewing for two separate "marketing jobs" that were actually pyramid schemes. (On that note, don't trust any interviewer who says they're making big money and then makes you pay your own way at Wendy's.) I also showed up to another interview hungover and unaware of the position I'd actually applied for—yet against all odds, I still got hired. (I should note for the record that I'm not recommending that particular approach. At all.)

The main reason you need a job is to support yourself financially—let's not pretend otherwise. Yet there's so much nuance to work beyond "provides a paycheck." The worst jobs are draining and destructive, while the best ones lead you to new places, introduce you to lifelong friends, and teach you skills you never knew you were capable of mastering. Your career will have a substantial impact on the rest of your life, and each of your jobs will form some component of your future.

So let's gaze into the crystal ball, shall we? The first step in obtaining a job is applying to lots and lots and *lots* of jobs. So many jobs. Even more than however many you're picturing.

# Excuse Me, Sir, Have You Seen Any Jobs Around Here?

*Learning about openings, interpreting descriptions, and networking (yes, networking!)*

Dear Businesslady,

My parents keep bugging me for job-search updates and I have no idea what to tell them. I mean, I get on Craigslist every couple of days and see what's posted recently in a handful of areas I'm interested in, but it's all so overwhelming and I feel like half the posts are scams anyway. I've got a decent amount of random experience from internships and other stuff I did in college (oversight roles in theater, sports clubs, etc.) so I think I'd be good at event planning or project management. Those are such broad categories, though, and I don't know how to find jobs I'd actually be qualified for, if they're even out there.

I know you're supposed to apply for as many jobs as possible, but I don't want to apply for EVERY position and hope for the best. How do people find viable job openings? And please don't say "networking" because I'm way too awkward for that.

—Desperately Seeking Something

➡ Even before you get to the complicated business of actually applying for jobs (and all the rigmarole that follows), you have to look at a job posting and think, "Hey, that's something I might be able to do." Before *that*, you have to weed through fafillions of other postings that are clearly looking for Not-You. A certain degree of desperation pretty much comes with the territory, but persevere! A determined and well-executed job search will eventually result in employment. Also, "networking" is just secret business-world code for "interacting with people you know"—so I have complete faith in your ability to deal.

## Preparing for the Hunt

Before you go on the prowl for job postings, take a moment to think about what you'd like to do—and be as idealistic as possible without resorting to "internationally famous unicorn groomer." Keep in mind that if you're being paid to do a thing, it's got to be something that other people find unpleasant/time-consuming/whatever enough to avoid doing themselves. So what are you good at that other people find daunting? What kind of tasks do you enjoy?

For me, I always loved editing, writing, and other forms of word nerdery. I was nearly thirty by the time I actually had "writer" in my job title, but those skills are the ones that helped me get hired and get promoted. For you, the answer could be motivating people, or organizing big projects, or tracking finances, or anything else that has a vague overlap with the needs of the working world.

If you're reading this and thinking "But I'm not good at *any*-thing," then first of all, hush, because that can't possibly be true. Secondly, you can also think about this from the inverse: what do you absolutely loathe, or what are you terrible at? Obviously the more of those things you can eliminate, the better.

Keep in mind, though, that if you're new to the workforce and/or eager to find a position as quickly as possible, you'll need to be flexible about which opportunities you consider. You can't get hired at a job you don't apply for, so save your choosiness for the offer stage.

### Surveying the Scene

You can find job listings in a lot of places—Craigslist will apparently be around until the heat death of the universe while others come and go, but Monster, CareerBuilder, and Indeed all seem to have staying power. Depending on your interests and background, there may be an industry-specific place for you to check (e.g., Idealist if you're interested in nonprofit work), and your local newspaper likely has an online "jobs" section. Beyond that, ask your friends, mentors, and Google for guidance on where to look based on what you're hoping to find.

Additionally, most organizations list open positions on their websites (although the "careers" or "employment opportunities" section is often buried in a weird spot, as though testing your ability to find it is part of their candidate-evaluation process). If there are particular places you'd like to work, see if they're hiring—the fact that you specifically sought them out helps demonstrate your passion and enthusiasm. (But don't go overboard. They're still going to be primarily interested in what you have to offer, and "deep and abiding love for Your Brand" isn't an actual qualification.)

### Acquiring Your Targets

As you're looking through job ads, you'll start to see commonalities: words like "required" versus "preferred," and desired skills or experience. It can feel discouraging when the list of attributes seems far removed from your own personal profile, but keep in mind that postings are wish lists. You probably won't land your ultimate fantasy dream job, and likewise, employers know that they're probably not going to get their ideal candidate. They're just trying to include enough detail to ensure that if their ideal candidate *does* exist, they'll be compelled to apply.

You don't have to be exactly what an organization is looking for, but there needs to be enough overlap between your qualifications and their needs that they'd plausibly want to interview you. If they require something that you don't have at all—say, a master's degree when you only have a bachelor's—then it's probably best to skip that position unless you can come up with a truly compelling reason why you're the exception (and even then, the odds are against you).

Some "requirements" are a bit less cut-and-dried, however. If they want "minimum 3 years of experience" and you have 2.5, that's close enough. Or if they're looking for proficiency with a particular kind of software, and you've never used it, you might be able to get around that by proving that you've quickly mastered a bunch of similar programs.

Instead of assessing each line of the description individually, try to get more of a big-picture sense of what they need and compare that to your own background. It's not an exact science, but in time you'll start to get a feel for the type of candidate you are and the types of jobs that are a good fit.

I'll get into actual applications in a bit, but as you're deciding which positions to pursue, keep this in mind: you need to be able to explain why you'd be good at everything you apply for—and that explanation needs to be legit, argument-and-evidence kind of stuff, not wishful thinking.

### Networking (Wait, Come Back!) and Informational Interviews

In addition to tracking down job postings through aggregator sites and individual listings, consider the amazing resource that is: the people you already know. Other humans can be a great source of intel, possibly even giving you inside access to whoever's in charge of hiring. Talking with those people regarding career stuff is known as "networking," which I think gets a bad rap because it's unfairly conflated with the idea of "using" your connections in a manipulative way—and, sometimes people kinda botch it, which contributes to the misconception that it's the worst.

You need to be thoughtful about how you're communicating and respectful of the other person's time—in networking and in all intrapersonal interactions, ideally. E-mailing (let's say) a friend's parent who works at a place where you're applying shouldn't feel any more conceptually gross than e-mailing someone who used to live in Barcelona about your upcoming vacation there. It is absolutely okay to ask "is your company hiring?" or "could you give me feedback on my resume?" or "could you pass my application on to this manager you know?" Be succinct, be gracious, take "no" for an answer—but don't let your personal sense of awkwardness keep you from becoming the friend-of-a-friend whose application ends up getting an extra push.

If you know someone who's in a job you'd love to have someday, or who otherwise represents the type of person you want to be when you grow up, you can go one step further and ask them for an informational interview. However, let's keep in mind WHAT AN INFORMATIONAL INTERVIEW IS NOT: it is not a secret job interview, nor is it an opportunity for you to waste someone's time by sitting there staring at them. Having a conversation won't magically make a job opening appear and put you in first-place contention, and merely being in someone's presence (or corresponding with them, or talking with them on the phone) will not provide you with any useful information about how they built their career. However, if you have an actual set of questions that you'd like answers to, it can't hurt to ask people whose input might be valuable. Even if they turn you down, you'll survive.

And so, onward! Finding job openings and networking won't do you much good if you don't actually get some applications out into the world.

# Selling Yourself Without Selling Out

*Creating a kick-ass resume—even
with a rocky job history*

Dear Businesslady,

My job history is the resume equivalent of turning your purse upside down and dumping out the contents. I've been a hairstylist, I've been a Disney theme park performer, I've done marketing for a failed startup, and I used to run a citywide social bike-riding organization. All of these experiences have been great and, I think, really educational, but it's impossible to put it all on paper in a way that convinces employers I'm worth talking to.

I used to be the part-time secretary for a small law firm in my hometown, so that's at least one "traditional" position. That was years before this other stuff, though, and I know that if your resume isn't chronological it's considered sketchy somehow (although I don't really understand why . . . ?). Anyway, I paid to have it professionally rewritten but all I got in return was a file with complicated formatting I can't figure out how to change. I'm ready to settle down and work a steady job, and I know I have a lot to offer, but I have no idea how to get any of it across in resume form.

—Jane of Too Many Trades

➤ The task of creating a resume can seem insurmountably daunting even if your work history is less eclectic than Jane's. The document itself feels so strange if you're not used to it: what do you list, and why, and who cares? I get that. Nevertheless, it's almost impossible to get hired anywhere without a resume—so you can either have a crappy, thrown-together one or one that actually helps you. I recommend the latter.

(Oh, and FYI for fancy folk—it's "résumé," with two accents.)

## Resumes: Work-You at a Glance

I definitely used to think resumes were just some weird ritualistic part of the job-search process that served no actual purpose. Now that I've been on the hiring side of things, I feel way, way differently. For almost any job opening, there are a huge number of applicants—far more than a manager could ever interview or even phone-screen. So how on earth does anyone make a decision? By scanning resumes. There's no better way to quickly assess someone's background in light of whether or not they can perform a particular job. (The other piece of the puzzle is the cover letter—and we'll tackle those next.)

As you're working on your resume, keep that audience in mind: the poor resume reviewer, overburdened, flooded with hundreds of pages of work histories, eyes glazing over but desperate for a glimmer of hope.

You're under no obligation to list every single job you've ever had, and in fact you *should* be adapting each resume you submit to the specific position you're pursuing. Tailor that shit! Make sure they can't miss what you need them to see.

Even so, it's true that you have to keep some amount of chronological detail in there or else it gets too hard to determine what you've been up to. If you just list jobs without dates, it's not clear whether you're a reliable person who sticks around long-term, or someone who quits at a moment's notice—or whether your relevant experience is recent, or decades out of date.

Rather than thinking of your resume as a kind of Permanent Record of every professional-ish thing you've ever done, think of it as a set of building blocks that can be infinitely recombined depending on the story you're trying to tell.

## Now, What Does That Mean in Practice?

For Jane, if she's applying for an admin role, she'll want to highlight her law-firm experience along with some of the oversight duties that were part of her bike-organization directorship. That doesn't mean she has to cut everything else, though—it demonstrates the breadth of her work history, however unconventional. So how should it all be organized? The best option is to include a "relevant experience" section, followed by "other experience."

Everything that's on your resume should be accompanied by some indication of the dates you held the job. For deep-history stuff, you can just list years if you want, but month + year is more informative (after all, "2011–12" could mean December 2011 through February 2012, or February 2011 through December 2012—and obviously those are very different lengths of time). For each position, include enough detail that it will make sense to an uninitiated person—a bunch of acronyms or strange industry-specific jargon will just be confusing and frustrating. If it's not clear where you worked and what you did, then you're just wasting space.

Here's what a resume should look like, from top to bottom:

- **Contact info** (e-mail and phone at a minimum, mailing address if so inclined—and make sure that the e-mail address is of the basic permutation-of-name variety).
- **"Skills summary"** or similar (a quick bulleted list of the stuff you're good at, adjusted to align with the position you're applying for).
- **Work history.** If you've got a lot of relevant experience, you might not want to even bother including the more tangential stuff—but then again, sometimes it can be interesting and a good conversation-starter at interview time. So assess this based on the story you're trying to tell with your cover letter, whether your officially unrelated experience might be meaningful to a hiring manager, and how much room you have.

- **Within work history:** a list of your responsibilities in each position. Not just job duties, but things you actually did, with specifics—and ideally, you can include a separate "achievements" section for things you did especially well. Instead of "designed brochures," say something like "brochure redesign: created artwork, organized layout, and produced new content in consultation with various stakeholders," and then further down, "improved brochures helped foster a 15% increase in enrollment." The more concrete detail, the better. Use present-tense for ongoing work, past-tense for everything else.
- **Education.** If you're fresh out of college and "person with a bachelor's degree" is one of your most significant professional selling points, that can go closer to the top, but eventually it should be relocated to the end (and at some point your GPA should be omitted, no matter how stellar it was—let's say a couple of years after graduation, or whenever interacting with college students makes you feel old). Any professional-development classes you've taken can go here too, along with pertinent training or formal certifications.
- **(Optional) Volunteering, etc.** The bottom of your resume is for anything else you want to include that falls outside of the aforementioned categories. Don't get too cute or too off-topic, though—keep it profesh.

Now, different industries have different norms, so if you're getting advice that vehemently contradicts this from trusted sources, it's worth considering. But at the same time, misinformation about resume construction is as tenacious as it is plentiful, so don't assume that one person's opinion is necessarily correct (even if that person works for your school's career center). For example, you'll sometimes hear that a one-page resume is mandatory, but that's ridiculous—it's fine to take up two pages if you have enough info to fill it out. That said, it *is* silly to have a second page that's only a line or two, or a two-page resume where half the content is filler.

Some folks prefer a sleek, streamlined resume, contributing to the prevalence of the one-page myth. That style can indeed be effective if you're further along in your career, with a series of fancypants titles that speak for themselves. But personally, I like more backstory. And if you don't yet have a history of impressively self-explanatory positions, you need to distinguish yourself from other applicants whose experience resembles yours—which means detailing the things that you, personally, have accomplished.

## For Future Reference

You'll notice that the resume items I've outlined don't include the phrase "References available upon request," and that was intentional. It goes without saying that you'll provide references if asked for them, so that's just wasting space—you might as well say "If you call me in for an interview, I won't refuse to talk to you like some kind of weirdo."

But while we're on the subject, references should be people who've actually managed you, which is to say former bosses. If you don't have many of those—or if you do but they're all in a completely different field than the one you're targeting—then you can list college professors or volunteer coordinators or people like that. ("People like that" ≠ a friend or relative, because they're biased—like, of course your *mom* is gonna say how great you are.) Your references should be people you've worked with extensively, though, since the bar for "was a good student" or "didn't actively screw up this volunteer project" can be considerably lower than the bar for "was a productive employee."

## It's Fine If It "Looks Like a Resume"

Finally, don't feel the need to get too elaborate with font, layout, or other formatting stuff. If you're a design geek who wants to do something interesting, go for it—but keep it readable. Your primary font should be black, any shading or graphics should be compatible with being printed on a black-and-white printer, and nothing should be too big or too small. *Nothing* should be too small. If you're trying to keep it to one page via .0001" margins and 8-point fonts, consider embracing a longer document: you don't want someone's first impression of you as a job candidate to be "whoa, this hurts my eyes."

In addition to the readability benefits, simple formatting will make it easier for you to rearrange sections and highlight different skills. I enjoy proofreading enough that I frequently help friends and friends-of-friends with their resumes, and anytime I get one that's based on one of those online template services, I get real frustrated real fast. Having a unique bullet-point shape and slightly unusual spacing isn't terribly helpful, but having a resume that gets totally messed up every time you change anything is actively *un*helpful. A resume that you're afraid to touch because of its complicated layout is a resume that you're not going to be tailoring enough.

On another mundane-yet-important practical note, don't forget that your resume's filename is going to be visible if you're applying electronically. No one's gonna *judge* you on it, but it's smart to go with some combo of your last name and the word "resume," without anything else that could be distracting (or embarrassing). And submit it in PDF so that your carefully arranged layout isn't destroyed by the vagaries of different operating systems.

In conclusion: a resume is a succinct outline of what you have to offer as an employee, pitched to whoever you're hoping will hire you. It needs to be accurate and honest, but also the most impressive possible reflection of your background. It's the beat and bassline of your work history, with the cover letter serving as the melody.

# Dear Hiring Manager

*Writing a great cover letter that
showcases your strengths*

Dear Businesslady,

I'm about to graduate from college and so, so eager to transition from working at a clothing store to something a little more "grown-up." But I'm freaking out because all of my friends studied business stuff and now they're just blithely moving from their high-paying internships to high-paying jobs at the same companies. (Okay, maybe I'm exaggerating a little, but that's how it feels.) I majored in sculpture and creative writing and I'm pretty sure no one will ever want to hire me for anything. But I'm smart and a hard worker and I swear I'd be good at officey things. How do I prove that I'm worthy of an entry-level job?

—Underemployed and Frantic

There are two answers to this question. The first is "you can't," and the second is "with a good cover letter." There are no guarantees in hiring—no matter how perfectly qualified you are for a job, you still might not make the cut. And no matter how impressive and comprehensive your resume is, it's not going to provide a complete picture of who you are as a real person and hypothetical employee. That's where the cover letter comes in.

## Write What You Know

A cover letter is a personal essay designed to convey your professional strengths. It's not a recap of your resume, but a supplemental document that helps provide context and depth beyond the bullet points.

Presumably you've written an argumentative paper at some point in your life, so think of "why I'd be a good fit for this job" as your cover letter's thesis. You've also probably heard the adage of "show, don't tell" in writing and that applies here too. "I'm smart and a hard worker and I swear I'd be good at officey things" isn't terribly convincing—just because you write something doesn't make it true. But if you provide examples of smart things you've done, ways your hard work was recognized, contributions you made to an office environment (or whatever the closest analog is from your experience), you'll pique someone's interest eventually.

It's tempting, especially when you're just starting out in your career, to try to counteract your youth by adopting the stuffiest possible voice—a kind of "drag" version of professionalism. Don't do that. (I definitely did, and I cringe when I look back at those old letters.) You do want to seem polished, though, which means adhering to time-honored conventions of grammar, syntax, and so on. For example, the tone of this book is probably a bit too breezy for a cover letter (and for that matter, its vocabulary isn't always the most work-appropriate). Still, it's closer to the ideal than "Forthwith I shall detail to you my most estimable businesswise proficiencies." You don't have to pretend to be someone you're not. It's fine to use a contraction (or two! go nuts!), or interject some humor if the opportunity arises.

The character you're playing in a cover letter is a version of yourself that's aligned with the position you're pursuing. If your background is a bit mismatched with the job description, the cover letter can help you overcome that. For example, while some aspects of retail work don't necessarily overlap with the business world, the ability to cheerfully deal with agitated people is a valuable skill whether they're customers or colleagues, so that's worth highlighting. Similarly, if there's something about your resume that you think might be a turnoff for employers, you can use the cover letter to address it up-front and put a positive spin on it.

## . . . But Don't Write Too Much

Your cover letter shouldn't be longer than a page, with an 11-point-minimum font and normal (i.e., 1") margins. Put paragraph breaks every 100-ish words—at logical pause points—so that readers aren't confronted by a wall of undifferentiated text. You should start with some invocation of the position you're applying for, and conclude with a "thanks for the consideration"–type sign-off. It's fine if you don't have a full page's worth of content in you, but you want at least 300 words' worth of prose (approximately) or else you're not making the fullest use of the hiring manager's attention.

The middle part is entirely up to you, and largely dependent on the specific alchemy between "You, Candidate" and the job description you're responding to. Oh yeah, that job description? Have it right in front of you as you're writing. You don't need to obsessively match up your words with their terminology, but the more you can hit the various beats of the ad—and match those beats with examples drawn from your own particular background—the more compelling it will be. The message is: I am the solution to your problems, and here's the evidence to support that claim.

Underscoring your professional qualifications is the entire point of the cover letter. It's great to show some personality, but it has to be in the service of your primary goal and that thesis of "why you should hire me." There may be things about a particular job that appeal to you—the commute, your eagerness to work in a given industry, whatever—but those are totally irrelevant from a hiring manager's perspective. I see a lot of "this job would allow me to gain valuable experience in [skill]" and to that I think, "I don't really give a shit about helping you gain experience—no offense." I understand the impulse behind statements like that, but they need a little bit of reframing in order to be effective.

Try this: instead of talking about how the job would be beneficial to *you* (even though that's the logical starting point from your own perspective), talk about the ways your enthusiasm will make you a more dedicated employee. Rather than saying you enjoy a particular kind of work, explain how you do it better or differently than other people and why that makes you more productive.

### Why Me?

Your application is going to be among dozens, if not hundreds, of others, and hiring managers are looking for any reason to weed you out. I'm not going to reject an otherwise stellar candidate over a misconjugated verb, but I would reject a lackluster candidate for one. What's the distinction between those two applicants? It often comes down to experience, sure. But you usually have to talk to someone before you can decide if they're right for the role, and reading cover letters and resumes helps you decide who you want to talk to.

Unlike resumes, which at best are pretty boring by design, cover letters offer a first glimpse into what someone might be like as a colleague—an actual human and not a list of skills. They answer questions like, Do I want to work alongside this person? Do I want to train them, manage them, mentor them? Will they fit in well here, will they be happy, will they stick around long-term? As a candidate, you can't know whether you're right for any given job or office, but if you present yourself authentically—and in a positive light—you'll get noticed by places where you'd be a good fit.

I already said you should refer to the job description as you're writing, but I can't emphasize that enough. If job-searching is like dating, then a cover letter is like the message you send after checking out someone's profile. That message can be an identical "sup" for every single person you find remotely attractive, or it can be "Wow, you're into *Obscure Cult Movie* too? [quotation of your favorite line]." The latter approach isn't necessarily going to get you partnered, laid, or even asked out on a date—but you're going to have more success that way than by carpet-bombing everyone with something generic.

It takes longer to write a good, tailored cover letter than a bland, all-purpose one. But you don't need to reinvent the wheel each time. Whenever you embark on a new application, look back at your previous cover letters, find the one that's the closest match, and then revise accordingly. Proofread it meticulously—under no circumstances should it contain vestiges of its previous life as a pitch for a different job—and then send it off.

After that, it's on to the next one. Most applications go nowhere, statistically speaking, so they're kind of like raffle tickets: the more you have out there, the better your odds.

With enough time and a little luck, you'll get called in for an interview. . . . which is a whole other thing.

# Tell Me About Yourself

*How to interview well—and maybe even have fun in the process*

Dear Businesslady,

Help! I have a job interview in two days but I have no idea how to job interview. My only other positions have been waitstaff jobs where you get hired on the spot after having a long enough conversation to assure the manager that you're not actively on drugs. I know I need to answer "what's your greatest weakness" with something that's secretly positive and that I should ask for the position at the end, but beyond that I'm totally clueless. To make matters worse, this is an interview for a job I *really* want—it's the perfect first step for where I want my career to go. It's also super competitive, so I need to make a good impression and really stand out.

Should I bring the interviewer a gift? How early do I need to get there? What am I going to *wear*?!

—Oh God, I Have to Buy a Suit Now, Don't I??

➡ Oh, the job interview. I've gotten to the point in my career where I actually enjoy these odd little interpersonal exercises, but I definitely remember a time when I felt just like Suit—right down to the misconceptions she voices about how to make a good impression. (Hint: under no circumstances should you bring a gift.) Interviews can be nerve-wracking, even for nerds like me who can get some pleasure out of them, but they don't have to be scary—I promise.

### Prepwork

When talking to a prospective employer, you don't want to be caught off-guard in a way that's easily avoidable—so avoid it. Go on the organization's website and review any and all "about us"–type content you can find, along with other info that's relevant to your particular position (like, if you're applying for a job running their Facebook page, it's probably a good idea to have . . . looked at their Facebook page). Reread the resume and cover letter you submitted so that your interviewer's reference materials are equally fresh in your own mind. Do a quick search to see if the company's been mentioned in the news lately or has any upcoming/recent events that you'll want to be aware of.

Basically, make sure that you won't seem totally clueless about who you're talking with, because that's a surefire way to accidentally imply that you're not actually that interested in the job. Once you've done your research, then you're ready to start interviewing.

### Phone/Video Screens:
### The First of Many Trials

Some employers will schedule an in-person interview right after reviewing your application, but it's pretty common to conduct a phone interview or "phone screen" before they meet you face-to-face. In terms of how you comport yourself, the discussion itself should be identical to the one you'd have in person, so what I say next still applies. But there are a couple of phone-specific details worth mentioning.

If a prospective employer contacts you at a bad time and you happen to pick up, that's okay! You're allowed to have a life beyond waiting for your phone to ring. Just don't try to have an interview at Six Flags because you feel bad asking someone to call you back.

Schedule the call when you know you'll be available, and then make sure you're in a quiet place with a well-charged phone at the appointed time. If some horrible confluence of disasters means you end up missing each other, follow up ASAP with abject contrition and see if you can get a second chance. (Phone interviews come with an unavoidable potential for technical difficulties, so you might get a single-use pass on being unavailable. Failing to show up for an in-person appointment, by contrast, is pretty much unforgivable.)

Again, for the love of any and all higher powers, do NOT try to participate in a phone interview while doing anything else. Don't be out shopping, don't be hunched in the stairwell in your office where your boss could walk by at any minute, don't be driving around. By multitasking during that call, you're saying, "this job is not a high priority for me" and your interviewer will think, "duly noted, happy to take you out of the running."

It's a little less likely that you'll be asked to participate in a video call as a first step, but it's a possibility, especially if you're applying for jobs beyond your immediate geographic area. Read on for guidance on how to handle the talking and self-presentation part (and yes, you should dress for a Skype interview like you'd dress for an IRL one, including whatever you wear below the waist). When connecting via the magic of technology, make sure you're somewhere quiet and distraction-free, with a simple (and not unprofessional!) background behind you. During the call, as much as you'll want to look at the person interviewing you and/or your own tiny little face, try to drag your eyes away from the screen—staring straight at the camera will give the impression of "eye contact" and will also save you from the distraction of worrying over your own expressions. Again, if you're stymied by technical difficulties, be apologetic and try to avoid the same problem if you manage to reschedule.

Once these initial discussions go well, you'll advance to the second round, which is usually an in-person interview.

## Looking the Part

Chronologically speaking, you have to get dressed before you show up at the interview site, so let's start there. And yes, in most cases (most jobs, most industries, most regions of the United States, etc.) you should wear a suit.

Ughhh, I know, what a pain. But interviews are an all-too-brief opportunity to present yourself to a potential employer, and "how you decided to dress" will be one of the few pieces of information your interviewer has about you.

Again, to draw on my favorite job-searching/dating metaphor, think about showing up to meet a potential paramour and seeing that they've worn straight-up pajamas to a decent restaurant. Now there may be people whose reaction would be "sweet, someone who loves PJs as much as I do!" or who truly wouldn't care about that particular fashion decision, and no judgment there. But for most of us, it would introduce a degree of "oh . . . kay, that's an interesting choice" that our date would have to overcome.

As a general principle, I'm against assessing people based on their clothing, but at an interview it's just part of the game. You can rebel against that reality if you'd like (and if you're chafing at this whole "wear a suit" idea, I have a feeling you'll find the upcoming "Wardrobe Assumptions" section worth reading), but them's the rules.

So: wear a suit. Rest assured that it probably doesn't have to be super fancy in order to be an acceptable interview uniform. When I say "suit," I basically mean "blazer plus same-colored bottom attire"—which could be a skirt or pants depending on your preference. Since black usually matches black, you can probably get a black blazer and then DIY a suit by pairing it with whatever black skirts/pants you already have. (Just be sure to check yourself out in a variety of lighting situations to make sure you haven't stumbled upon a mismatch—if you inadvertently pair a purply black with a greenish black, that'll ruin the illusion of unity.) Or you can shop around until you spot an inexpensive work-appropriate ensemble in black, charcoal grey, or another similarly neutral shade—those are all versatile, and conservative enough to fit the bill at stodgier employers. (Anyone looking to get a job in a highly fashion-conscious industry will probably have to work a little harder to present well, but I doubt that comes as a surprise.)

Thinking back, I actually don't know if I even owned a suit when I was fresh out of college, so clearly there's some flexibility beyond what I'm suggesting. But even if you're way overdressed for an interview, that—at worst—suggests "I'm really trying here." Which is endearing. Whereas if you go with a more casual look and your interviewer is a hard adherent of the Interview=Suit school of thought, you're starting off at a minor disadvantage.

For the suit-averse or financially strapped, at the very least you should wear your most professional-looking outfit. That doesn't mean your *fanciest* outfit, so if it's something you'd wear to the proverbial club, it's unlikely to do effective double-duty as interview attire. You don't need to completely abandon your usual fashion sense, but dial it a couple of notches toward the conservative. Think grandparent-visiting, funeral-attending, etc. Make sure you look "polished," whatever that means for you—nothing wrinkled, raggedy, stained, unkempt, whatever. You don't need to get a manicure if you don't normally get manicures or wear makeup if you otherwise never wear makeup, but whatever your A+ grooming game is, do that. You can slowly morph into the shlubbier version of yourself once you've got the job.

### Get Me to the Office On Time

Your teeth are brushed and you look like a professional-esque version of yourself, so now it's time to head out the door to your interview.

That's assuming you're leaving from home, of course. If you're already employed and interviewing, you might have to field questions from coworkers about "why are you so dressed up" or—if you've got a super-casual dress code at your workplace—follow the time-honored tradition of changing into a suit in a Starbucks bathroom without getting too flustered by the indignity of it all.

Regardless of where you're starting from, you'll have to get to where you're going—and you really, really, *really* don't want to be late. (That should go without saying.) But early can be bad too—more than ten minutes and it gets awkward to have someone chilling in the front lobby with nothing to do. That puts you in the somewhat unmanageable position of allowing enough travel time to overcome even the most catastrophic traffic or public-transit malfunctions while also not showing up way too soon. As you're scouting your destination, see if there's a coffee shop or similar neutral space nearby where you can camp out and burn off your buffer time. (Or if you're driving, you can sit in the car until you hit that not-too-early sweet spot.)

Once you arrive, feel free to graciously accept whatever beverages you're offered, or decline if you'd prefer. Ask where the bathroom is if you need a pit stop before you go in. The goal is to be as prepared as you can possibly be when the scheduled time rolls around, whatever that entails.

Oh, and be nice to the receptionist. (That goes without saying too, right? Because you're basically a nice person?) As someone who's been the first point of contact for job candidates, I can confirm that higher-ups will hear about it if you're a jerk. From the moment you enter the office, you're being evaluated to some extent, and that doesn't end until you're well out of earshot. Don't overthink it, but do be on your best behavior.

### The Conversation

After all this sartorial and transportational to-do, you'll reach the moment where some human will emerge from the depths of the office and say your name in a questioning tone. You'll give 'em some amiable eye contact and a firm (but not death-grip) handshake, and with that, your interview is officially underway.

The person sitting across from you at a job interview should, at some point, be the manager you'd report to if you got the job. That's not necessarily the first person you'll speak with, though, which means that you might end up interviewing with someone who doesn't actually know a lot about the position. Or they might be perfectly well-informed, but terrible at interviewing.

I've had interviews that felt like a true meeting of the minds, full of back and forth. The questions were all, "how would you handle something like ____?" which gave me the opportunity to say "well, in those types of situations I usually ____" and so on. That's the ideal.

But I've also had interviews where I had to awkwardly interrupt a litany of minutiae about the office and position in order to pipe up with some info about why I might be qualified. Just because you leave an interview feeling defeated and frustrated doesn't necessarily mean you did anything wrong. And if your interviewer seems like they don't know what they're doing, that's probably because they don't! You're allowed to try to redirect their rambling monologue, and an interviewer who's struggling might be grateful for a segue like "You know, I dealt with something similar at [last job] and I handled it by [doing some awesome thing that's relevant to this new role]."

In general, that "what I've done/how it might help you" format is what you're striving for with everything that comes out of your mouth during an interview. You don't have to be a self-promotion robot—it's fine to let the conversation unfold naturally and have human moments of connection like "Oh, I love that band too." But just because you and your interviewer become BFFs doesn't mean you'll get a callback or an offer. Bad interviewing can take many forms, and a chatty discussion of everything *but* your suitability for the role isn't serving any meaningful assessment purpose. Just like with your resume and cover letter, you should take every opportunity to explain what you have to offer.

A good interviewer will ask a lot of pointed questions, like "tell me about a time when you did ____" where that blank is something specific and job-related. You want to be prepared to respond with equally specific answers. Not "I talked to my coworkers and, I don't know, figured it out" but "I took an informal survey of the various departments' needs and came up with a cost-effective solution." Plus even more details than that (which of course I can't really formulate as a hypothetical example). If you get asked about something you've never encountered before, speculate on how you *would* deal with that thing—and if you can draw on a related accomplishment in the process, so much the better.

Since interviewing is about figuring out the fit between a candidate and a position, questions like "what's your biggest weakness?" are of dubious value—something like "what do you struggle with the most?" is going to be a lot more instructive. But one way or another, a competent interviewer is going to try to assess your shortcomings, and unless they're intensely gullible they're going to see right through bullshit like "If I have one flaw, it's that I love working too much." I mean, to return to the dating analogy again, if someone said their past relationships all ended because "I'm just too loving and supportive of my partners," you'd roll your eyes, then bail—whereas "I can be really critical and sometimes that makes me tough to live with" is actually enlightening.

You don't need to overshare or use the interview as an opportunity to confess your biggest professional blunders, but being up-front about your own strengths and weaknesses demonstrates thoughtfulness and honesty. It'll also help you stand out from anyone else who did opt for a silly "my weakness is secretly a strength" approach. There actually *are* negative consequences to supposedly positive traits: being accommodating vs. being a pushover, being meticulous vs. taking forever to get things done, being rigorous about process vs. being inflexible if there's a need for change, and so on.

Everyone's skills and flaws are on a continuum, so you can use that to contextualize your more problematic qualities and convey how you're trying to improve. As in: "I pride myself on being helpful, so I find it hard to say 'no' when I'm asked to do things—but then this causes problems with my workload because I don't have time for everything I've committed myself to. I'm trying to enforce better boundaries and work with my manager to set priorities so I can respectfully decline certain tasks while maintaining my reputation as someone who's willing to go above and beyond." (If you just thought, "That actually *is* my weakness," then you'll enjoy Chapter 3, by the way.)

It's not uncommon to have several interviews with different people, so you may find yourself repeating The Saga of How I Improved Our Social Media Presence multiple times in the course of an afternoon. So be it. Eventually everyone you met with will get together and compare notes, but they're not going to recount your anecdotes verbatim, so treat each new sit-down as its own individual interview.

Beyond these major beats, the actual shape the interview will take depends on the role, your background, and the particular dynamic between you and the person (or people) you're talking to. Ideally you'll manage to provide a rich array of information about your skills, while simultaneously learning more about the role in question.

### Yes, You Have Questions for Them

You find yourself at an interview because you want a particular job (or think you do—more on that in a minute), and thus it's easy to assume that your end goal is a job offer. But that's not entirely correct. No matter how intently you review the job description, research the company, or otherwise prepare, you can't possibly know what the office is like, whether you'll click with your would-be manager, or what the actual day-to-day work will entail. Not all jobs are created equal, and if you think a terrible job is better than no job at all, you clearly haven't had a terrible job yet.

And yes, I realize that financial constraints often prevent candidates from being too picky. Taking a kinda-crappy job is definitely preferable to getting evicted—but you still want to know what specific type of crappiness you're signing up for, and the job interview is your chance to figure that out.

You can and absolutely should ask questions that will help you decide whether or not you'd thrive in the position: Is it a true 9-to-5 or do people usually stay late? What's the management style? Are there opportunities for advancement? Adjusted, of course, for what matters most to you. (Stay focused on the work itself, though—the interview isn't the place to bring up nitty-gritty details like vacation time, benefits, or specific scheduling requests.)

You might realize during the course of the interview that you actually *don't* want the job—that happens! You don't necessarily want to declare it outright, but you also don't have to feign enthusiasm you don't feel or gloss over any surprising new information you learn in the course of the discussion.

A lot of this dovetails with "finding your fit" more generally, which is coming up in the next section. For now, just remember that an interview is also a fact-finding mission. You're judging them as much as they're judging you, which hopefully will serve as an antidote against anxiety. You're still a person, and this is still a conversation. You've just got specific things you need to convey and another set of things you want to figure out.

### Thanks for Your Time; We'll Be in Touch

Your turn to ask questions usually comes at the end, when you and your interviewer are wrapping things up before you both get on with your day. It closes the loop on the information exchange, ensuring that neither one of you has any knowledge gaps that will impede your decision-making further along in the process.

One of those questions should *not* be "So do I get the job?" Even if everyone loved you, it's unlikely that they have the authority to hire you on the spot, so you're basically just inviting awkwardness by asking. But if you're genuinely excited about the position, it's fine to say as much. And even if the interview has made you more skeptical about whether or not you'd like working there, stick the landing by thanking your interviewer(s) warmly and ending things on a positive note.

After you've relocated to somewhere else, send thank-you e-mails to everyone you met with. If you didn't get everyone's contact info, e-mail whoever you can and include something about "please share my thanks with so-and-so too." (And if you didn't get everyone's *name*, well, whuups. Put it on the to-do list for next time.)

This note doesn't have to be lengthy, but it should reiterate your interest in the position (if that's true) and—if possible—mention something you discussed with your interviewer. You can e-mail everyone at once or send individual notes, depending on which seems most natural in the circumstances. Just send *something*, because it's part of the norms around interviewing and failure to follow up will signal disinterest.

After that, try as hard as you possibly can to pretend that the interview didn't happen. Anyone who's smart about hiring will be talking to lots of qualified candidates, and you can't know how you measure up to your competition—even if you felt like you absolutely crushed it. Statistically speaking, you're more likely to get rejected than hired, so steel yourself to that reality and move on. Think about what went well, what didn't, what you wish you'd done differently—write it down while it's fresh in your head and refer to those notes when you prep for future interviews (which you will get, I assure you). Most importantly, keep on sending out other applications, because your search isn't over until you actually get a job.

They know you're interested, and if they decide to hire you, it won't be because they sensed your anxious energy reverberating through the universe. If you absolutely must dwell on the possibility of an offer, use that time to develop a game plan for how you'll respond.

# From "a Job" to "Your Job"

*Assessing your options, evaluating your offers,
and finding your fit*

Dear Businesslady,

I'm a finalist for two different jobs, and I suspect they're both going to make me an offer. I've been trying to get hired for months, but now that things are finally coming together, I'm scared about what comes next.

I wish there was a clear frontrunner, but there's not. One of the jobs seems really cool (work I'm passionate about, I really connected with the people) but it'd be a crazy-long commute and they've made it clear they don't have much budget for staff salaries. The other one would pay a lot more and it's way closer, but the stuff I'd be doing seems less interesting.

I'm also assuming they also both have benefits that are . . . good? But I don't really know how to judge that, to be honest (I'm still on my parents' insurance!).

I know I'm not going to stay in this next job forever but I don't want to take something "okay" when I could be doing something that could make me really happy. Should I pick passion over paycheck or the other way around? I'm so afraid of making the wrong decision, especially when I'm not even sure what my priorities should be.

—Trying to Turn This Dilemma into Di-lemonade

➤ It's easy to get so caught up in the hope/disappointment cycle of the job search that you forget you're actually setting the stage for a life-changing decision. Even if you're not super career-focused, your job will be a huge part of your overall life experience (like it or not), so it's worth being thoughtful about what you're getting into. At the same time, there's not necessarily a single correct choice. As you're deliberating, just get as much information as you can and then make your peace with the outcome.

Beyond the ever-important salary—which we'll cover next—the major factors to consider when evaluating a job opportunity are the benefits, the organization's culture (and I'm including things like schedule and commute under that umbrella), and then finally—obviously—the actual work you'll be doing. That complexity makes it tough to directly compare different positions, but once you've thought carefully about each component, you should have a sense of how happy you'd be with any particular job.

### Review Your Interview Recon

It's pretty much impossible to get offered a professional office job without at least one interview, and while you can learn certain things about a place before visiting it in person, no organization's website is going to say "Our offices smell weird and we don't have nearly enough space." While you're onsite, pay close attention to all the ambient data available to you, along with everything else about the pre-offer experience. Do the people in the office seem frazzled, happy, bored? Has their hiring process seemed organized or chaotic? Do you get the sense that your interviewer is being sincere or lying through their teeth? Combined, all of these signals create a comprehensive picture of what the job will actually be like in the day-to-day. Don't ignore your intuitions.

### Friends with Benefits

Unless you have very specific needs (medical, educational, etc.) or are weighing two nearly identical job offers, it's unlikely that benefits will be the deciding factor in and of themselves. Nevertheless, they're still an important part of your overall compensation.

It's understandable that you'll want more info about things like benefits, time off, specific scheduling, and so on before deciding to accept a position, but conventions dictate that you can't ask about that stuff until you have an offer in hand. So for the purposes of this section, let's pretend you've gotten The Call and learned that they'd like to hire you—even though you might start investigating some of these things in advance of that conversation. (More on the actual logistics of that call and your response are coming right up.) Most largish companies will have information about their benefits packages ready to go and can give it to you if you ask. And in general, the bigger the company, the better their insurance offerings, simply because they have more bargaining power.

For evaluation purposes, you'll want to look at the out-of-pocket cost to you, for both the insurance itself as well as copays. Maybe I was just an idiot, but I used to think that the health insurance you got through your job was totally free, when in fact that's rarely the case: you get a certain amount deducted from your paycheck based on the coverage you choose and whatever rate exists between your employer and the provider. Depending on the plan, there's wide variation in costs that are passed along to the employee. If the premium is really high, it affects your overall take-home pay, which is worth knowing—especially because you can't change that through negotiation, unlike your salary. And if you're going to be taking advantage of dental or vision coverage, that's usually separate from health insurance proper.

All of this can add up, so make sure you crunch the numbers. For example, a $40k/year job might seem dramatically better than a $34k/year job in terms of raw salary, but if you'd be paying $6k a year toward insurance in the first position and only $1k a year in the second, they start looking a lot more comparable.

Beyond insurance, other benefits an employer might offer include paid vacation/sick time (either individually or as part of one shared "time off" pool), some kind of retirement plan or stock options, and subsidies for things like public transit, education, or gym memberships. This is not a comprehensive list by any means. If an employer is particularly generous with its perks, that will be something they cite as a counterargument when you ask for a bigger paycheck—that's why those perks exist, to "add value" beyond salary alone (and often at a lower aggregate cost than giving each individual employee more money). But just because something is labeled a benefit on paper doesn't mean it's a benefit *to you*, so don't necessarily believe the hype. Of course, if every single perk is perfectly aligned with your lifestyle, then that could be worth a salary tradeoff—and a sign that you're a good fit for the organization's overall culture.

The bottom line: don't just smile and nod when you hear "we have great benefits." Ask to see something that explains what that actually means and then evaluate it accordingly.

### The Nitty and the Gritty

You're not obligated to have a litany of questions ready to go when you're contacted with an offer—but if you do, you can start asking them right away. Otherwise, it's better to schedule a follow-up conversation once you've had a chance to think things over, or to send an e-mail outlining the stuff you're curious about: "Thanks, I'm really excited about this opportunity, but I need a little while to consider it. Would you mind if I got back to you on [date]? In the meantime, I was wondering about . . ." Feel free to ask direct questions aimed at learning more about the job and the way it fits into the larger organization—although some people might prefer to respond via phone instead of e-mail if the answers are complicated (and you might want to explicitly offer "I'd be happy to discuss this by phone" as an option).

As you're talking through the offer, that's the time to bring up the logistical stuff you didn't address in the interview: Is it okay if you leave early once a week for a standing appointment? What's their work-from-home policy? Will it be okay for you to take time off a month in to attend a friend's wedding? Yes, in theory some of these might be deal-breakers—if you absolutely need to leave by 2 P.M. on Fridays and they have a long-standing all-staff meeting at 3 P.M., then they might decide to hire someone else rather than disrupt their system. But which is worse: to have the offer disintegrate or to show up on your first day and announce that you weren't actually up-front about your terms? (Or, put another way, if a company's policy was to deny all vacation requests for the first year, when would you want to find that out—while discussing the offer or whenever you tried to schedule some time off?)

In addition to these practical details, you can also address anything that's been giving you pause about the position: Is there a plan in place to get you trained on [unfamiliar software]? How long will it be before [coworker] position is filled, and how will that affect you in the meantime? Again, there might be a few outlier companies who have a "how dare you question us" mindset, but most good employers will want you to be well informed before you accept their offer.

### Commuting: Your Sentence

It may seem like a minor point in the grand scheme of things, but your commute is a major aspect of your workday. And even if you left from your home to go to your interview, that doesn't necessarily mean you've experienced that journey during the times you'll be traveling to and from your new office.

Now, if you live three blocks away, then you can safely assume you've got your commute research covered. But otherwise, I'd urge you to look up the public-transit or roadways-with-applicable-traffic route that would become your everyday reality. If you can swing it, doing a trial run will be even more instructive—it's one thing to see "45 minutes of gridlock" on an app screen and a very different thing to experience it firsthand with brutal regularity.

For someone who relishes the chance to spend quality time with podcasts, music, or (audio)books, a substantial commute might not be a problem. But if you know you get antsy whenever you're in transit for too long, don't pretend that's suddenly going to change just because you're employed.

### Mirror, Mirror on the Wall, What's the Best Job of Them All?

That "know thyself" rule applies to everything else about the position too. As you're processing all this information, weigh it against the vibe you got at the interview and the details you have about the actual tasks you'll be asked to accomplish. It's rare to find a job that's exactly what you were hoping for with zero drawbacks, so you'll probably have to decide whether the negatives outweigh the positives (and vice versa, and by how much). Your deliberation will need to factor in a bunch of other issues as well—the other options available to you, how badly you need a reliable source of income, and whatever activities and interests animate your non-work life. For the sake of argument, though, let's assume that you're lucky enough to be choosing from several viable possibilities.

With all the facts in evidence, sit down for some honest reflection about who you are and what you prioritize. Ideally you'll stick around in this job for at least a year, so you want to make sure you're ready to commit. Do you think you'll be happy with your role—good at it, fulfilled by it, challenged by it on a regular basis? (Or, if you're specifically hoping for something "easy," does this job hit the mark?) To whatever extent you have long-term career goals—and it's all right if you don't—how does this position align with those? Will the commute drive you nuts after a few months? Do you think you could make friends with at least a few coworkers (not mandatory, but an awesome bonus if it happens)? When you imagine saying "I work for _____," how do you feel?

You are the ultimate arbiter of whether or not any given job is right for you, but fortunately you're also the world's foremost expert on your own self—so use that knowledge to your advantage. Make pro and con lists, hash out your thoughts with trusted confidantes, and/or do whatever usually guides you through major choices. If you're still undecided, try flipping a coin—not to make the decision for you, but to help you figure out how you really feel (sometimes you don't realize you were rooting for "heads" until you see that it landed on "tails"). Eventually, you'll have your definitive answer.

It's certainly possible that said answer will be "I think I'm gonna hate this job but I really need it." Such is life for the non-rich. While it's better to have a resume full of long-term jobs, you can usually get away with a couple of short-term stints—particularly early in your career when you're still figuring things out. If you find yourself in the situation of taking a for-now job while holding out for a better one, go ahead and keep your job search active while you try to make the best of a less-than-ideal position. But you'll want to stay put for a while at your next gig, so finding a good fit will be even more important whenever you eventually move on.

At the very least, all this contemplation should lead you to a shortlist of "jobs I would be happy to take," perhaps with caveats attached like "if the pay is good enough." And once you've gotten that settled, it's time to make your salary as high as it can possibly be.

# Because You're Worth It

*Figuring out what you want and negotiating to your advantage*

Dear Businesslady,

I spent so much time desperately hoping for interviews, and then job offers, that I forgot to think about negotiating. Now I've finally gotten an offer for a job I think I want, and I'm completely stuck. Should I ask for more money, or will that risk pissing them off?

To complicate things, there's another position I'm even more excited about, but I haven't heard anything from them since my interview last month. Should I reach out to them and see if they're interested before I decide?

I want to make sure I'm not just slowly going into debt until (and unless) I get a major raise. But I also don't want to shoot myself in the foot by seeming greedy or unrealistic. Plus, I'm starting to realize I don't even know how negotiation actually works. Like, I know you should do it, but how do you actually start that conversation without seeming like a money-grubbing jerk?

—Don't Wanna Be a Sucker

➤ Talking about money is uncomfortable at best, but what if you combine it with the inherent stress of job-searching? Oh, right, then it only gets more unpleasant.

Given how rarely this comes up, it's tempting to just avoid the whole issue and accept whatever you're offered. That's easier from a certain standpoint, but it ultimately works against your own self-interest. If you don't want to be a sucker, you're going to have to suck it up and negotiate.

### You Have Been Chosen

The negotiation process starts with the offer itself, which will most likely happen via a phone call. (I know we're all eagerly rushing toward a future in which using telephones for communication is akin to using horses for transportation, but let's pretend for a second that talking isn't yet an antiquated medium.) If you see the call coming in, pick up if you're available, and if you can't, then call back as soon as possible. Yes, *call* them back.

Having this conversation voice-to-voice allows the manager to informally assess your enthusiasm, and it's also a more efficient way of establishing the timeline for your response and quickly talking through simple questions. Don't feel obligated to accept or decline on the spot—an evaluation period of at least a day or two (if not more) is standard. So even if you're completely blindsided, stammer out some version of "thanks, can I think this over and get back to you on [day]?" Be wary of jobs that try to strong-arm you into an immediate response. It's one thing if they need an answer within a specific time frame—especially if they offer some explanation for the urgency—but if they're pressuring you to answer instantaneously, it's likely because they're worried you'll decline if you give it more thought. And, uh, nope on that tactic.

### You're a Limited-Time Opportunity

In general, you want to leave prospective employers alone (except when submitting applications and scheduling interviews). But if you get a job offer while you're still in the running for other positions that you're equally—if not more—excited about, it's worth checking in with those places before proceeding. They'll probably respond with "we're not ready to make offers yet, sorry," but you might learn that you're already out of contention (which should help you feel more confident about accepting a different job), and there's a slim possibility that they *were* planning on hiring you, and that your nudge will help them accelerate their timeline. Plus, there's something just *satisfying* about contacting a place that was maybe going to reject you and letting them know—however politely and professionally—that you're wanted elsewhere.

### More Money, Less Problems

Back to your actual offer, and the biggest detail of all: salary. Unless it's been explained to you that there's absolutely NO flexibility on that front—attached to a believable rationale, like "our grant only allots so much money to this position"—you're doing yourself a disservice if you don't ask for more. We're talking about your livelihood here! If you think that negotiating an initial offer sounds difficult, trust me when I say that asking for a raise is so much harder, and way less likely to be successful. This is your one opportunity to increase your base income, and since future increases will be predicated on that initial amount, you should make the most of it.

Now, they may not bump up the amount just because you asked. And you probably don't want to play hardball, especially if you're fairly junior—in fact, if it's a truly entry-level job, it's likely that the response will be some variant of "you get what you get and you don't get upset." But the stakes only get higher as you get further along in your career, so if nothing else, you should seize these early offers as your chance to get comfortable with negotiating. Even if they hold firm on the original number, you'll be no worse off financially, and you'll have gained some experience in the process. You might feel awkward about it, but that will subside once you're on the job and the salary-talk interaction recedes into your past.

### Let's Be Reasonable

I'm resolutely pro-negotiation, but I'm also pro-not-being-stupid-about-it. Requesting a few extra thousand dollars isn't going to make anyone rescind your offer (even if they turn you down), and if they *do* reject you for attempting to negotiate, that's a red flag and a bullet dodged. On the other hand, if you ask for a salary that's wildly out of sync with the standards for your region, field, and skill level, then employers will understandably find it off-putting. You probably won't get an offer pulled for negotiating per se, but a gross overreach might signal "this person doesn't get it" and *that* could make them rethink hiring you.

So how do you figure out what's reasonable? You do your research: asking people you know in similar positions at similar organizations, reviewing the salary ranges in ads for similar jobs, and looking up pay data online (resources like Glassdoor and the U.S. Bureau of Labor Statistics can give you some general guidelines—although fair warning that they aren't always accurate or perfectly relevant). If there's a wide discrepancy between the offer you're expecting and the one you receive, you can ask for a significant pay bump—but you'll have to explain yourself (e.g., "I've noticed that the compensation for junior consultant roles is usually around X, so I was hoping for something closer to that").

Even if the offer is perfectly fair, you'll probably want to negotiate anyway, just so you get some practice for the next time when the stakes might be higher. But don't overdo it: ask for a smaller increase, say around 5 percent (or whatever amount feels right to you).

The one exception is for an unusually generous offer—if, say, you've indicated you'd be thrilled with $45k and they offer you $46k, then negotiating won't make you seem like an assertive go-getter, it'll make you seem inconsistent and greedy.

### You Can't Buy Happiness

We've already discussed all the other factors that go into your job satisfaction beyond your paycheck. Some of them can't be changed no matter how naturally persuasive you are ("Please relocate your offices so they're accessible by this train line" is not an actionable request), but others are more malleable than you might realize. While every workplace will be uncompromising on certain points, you won't know what options are available to you until you ask.

So, ask.

Wish you had a different title? See if that's a possibility. Psyched about a job but dreading one small aspect of it? See if you could get those duties taken off your plate. Hoping to arrange your schedule so that you miss the worst of rush hour or don't have to pay for extra daycare? See if they offer that kind of flexibility.

Of course, "I'd like an extra $6k *and* please give me a cooler title *and* how 'bout I work from home two days a week *and* I don't wanna do mail merges" isn't likely to go over well, so once you're armed with your list of needs, wants, and nice-to-haves, prioritize and use common sense.

## A Little Friendly Disagreement

Regardless of the particulars of your ideal negotiating outcome, it will boil down to some version of "I want more." And regardless of how accommodating an organization is, someone in their hierarchy will want to give you less. So there's an inherent conflict—but that doesn't mean inherent hostility. Throughout the negotiation you want to keep your tone cordial, professional, and warm, conveying "I'm so excited about this position . . . if only we could make these few small tweaks." If the discussion gets adversarial, then you may need to walk away from the job entirely. No one wants to hire someone who seems like they're being dragged on board against their will.

In theory, if a place is really eager to hire you, then your manager might do battle on your behalf to get you everything you've asked for. But that's rare. You're probably going to have to compromise, so before you begin the discussion, think about what's most important to you. Also think about what's *least* important to you (but still desirable), because that's something you can make a point of giving up in the interest of finding common ground. "Okay, I will magnanimously relinquish my desk by the window [which I don't actually care about] in exchange for the option of regularly working from home [which oh my god will make my life so much easier]." Just don't say the bracketed stuff *out loud*, and boom, you've done some strategic negotiating.

The random timing of the job-search process makes it unlikely that you'll have two open offers simultaneously, but if you find yourself in that position—and especially if you'd be happy with either—you can leverage one against the other. Just be especially careful about maintaining a positive tone, because otherwise you risk implying that one of them is your second choice (which is especially problematic if your first choice gets that impression). Your attitude should be "Oh, I would love like to accept a position with you—it's just that the terms of this other offer are so, so tempting!" and not "Why should I take your dumb job when this other company truly appreciates me?"

## The Showdown

Whenever you open the negotiation, you don't want to jump in immediately with Here's What I Want. A subtle approach makes it easier to keep things in the right emotional register, and since most managers (or HR reps, or whoever your primary point of contact is) will expect you to negotiate, they should realize what's happening even if you're not being blunt.

Start with your biggest priority, but formulate your request as an inquiry about possibilities instead of a demand: "is there any room to increase the salary a bit?," "I was wondering if you might be open to a title change," or "how flexible are you regarding employee schedules?" (You can tackle two priorities at once if both of those things are equally important to you, but no more than that.) If you get told "no," then you can either accept it or push back a bit: "I see; well, that's disappointing because I'd really be thrilled to accept this job if not for ____."

Be prepared to justify your wants and make a case for why you deserve them. When discussing salary, this argument should *not* concern your personal finances (as with your cover letter, your rationale shouldn't rely on anything that falls under the category of "why would your employer care?").

These factors *are* relevant to your salary, however:

- Market rates for your area
- Competitiveness with other jobs/offers
- Unusually high healthcare premiums
- Limited time off
- The complexity of the role and the talent required to do it well

Your previous salaries aren't necessarily relevant, but if you're already employed and the new job would constitute a pay cut, that's definitely worth mentioning.

Once you've talked through your #1 priority, chances are you'll have arrived at a resolution that's somewhere between their original offer and your request. That's when you move on to your lesser priorities, citing the disparity between what you wanted and what they ended up giving you. From there, the back-and-forth follows a similar pattern. As long as you don't get the sense that your employer-side contact is getting frustrated, and you're taking pains to reiterate your enthusiasm for the job throughout the discussion, you should be able to keep things appropriately friendly. (If you do start sensing frustration and you'd be happy with the existing offer, then you should quit while you're ahead—and if not, go ahead and keep pushing, because what do you have to lose?)

### Finally, Acceptance

Eventually, after the tense cordiality of the negotiation is over, you'll have a revised final offer. Some places will put it in writing right away, but often they're not willing to go through the hassle of preparing an actual document before you've agreed verbally. If you're accepting over the phone, make sure you're being clear about the terms: "With a salary of $39k and the title of Junior Awesomeness Consultant, plus the option to arrive late on Wednesdays like we discussed, I would be more than happy to accept. Thanks so much for working with me on those details."

After that, the written offer should just be a formality—but if you notice any discrepancies, flag those right away. (Particulars like scheduling agreements probably won't appear in the offer itself, but you can and should get them documented via e-mail.) If you agree to a salary and see a different number in print, that's not necessarily a sign that they're deliberately trying to screw you—it's probably just an innocent mistake or the result of a miscommunication—but if it's not corrected before you start, you might be stuck with that smaller paycheck forever.

If you get the written offer up-front, then your response should follow the same lines, expressing gratitude for their flexibility and your excitement about joining their team.

. . . you *are* excited, right? You should be, because you just got yourself a job—congratulations! Now you just have to figure out how to get through the couple-thousand hours a year you'll be spending there. Yay, work.

## CHAPTER 2

**LET'S DO THIS:**

# Starting (and Having) a Job

I DISTINCTLY REMEMBER showing up for my first office job and feeling like I was stepping off the plane in a foreign country—a faraway one in a different time zone where I couldn't speak or read the local language. Most of us enter the workforce in this kind of immersion-program way, where you just muddle along until you no longer feel like your entire body is made of pure, crystallized awkwardness. Eventually, it starts seeming pretty natural. And then you get another job and learn that one place's normal is another place's aberrant and vice versa.

So that's the big caveat for this section: every office is different. If you're following my advice to the letter but feel like you're not fitting in, trust the cues of your immediate environment.

With that disclaimer out of the way, my goal is to serve as the friendly tour guide for your arrival in the strange, exotic land of the professional workplace. It takes everyone a while to acclimate to a new position—to settle into a routine, find friends, and just generally feel comfortable. But that process is a lot easier once you have a map for navigating office life, and if you haven't experienced it firsthand, then a primer like this is your best shot at feeling well prepared on day one.

# How to Career, Part I

*What to expect—and not freak out about—
in an office environment*

Dear Businesslady,

I'm about to start my first office job and I'm starting to panic—not about the work part but everything else. Should I bring my lunch, or is that weird? Should I plan on going out for lunch, or is *that* weird? I want to be friendly with my coworkers but I don't know how—wandering up to people and starting conversations with them seems . . . well, weird. Again.

Is there, like, an instruction manual for people who have no idea what they're getting into when they show up in cubicle-land for the first time?

—Stranger in a Normal Land

➤ The most "normal" thing about office life is that everyone feels like an outsider on their first day of work. Still, while every place is going to have its own rhythms, unwritten rules, and strange quirks, there are a few commonalities—and, more importantly, a few things you can learn that will help you feel more comfortable more quickly.

### . . . And, You're Off

Starting a new job is a lot like going to an in-person interview, only (hopefully) a lot less stressful. You want to be on time—but not too early!—and you want your attire to err on the professional/conservative side (this time, informed by whatever you noticed other people wearing during your last visit). You want to bring along everything you'll need throughout the day (including sustenance—more on that in a bit), but you don't need to arrive armed with an entire box of desk decorations or anything; that stuff is best accumulated gradually once you've gotten a feel for the vibe of the place.

Mainly you just want to show up ready to learn like it's your job—because for the time being, it kind of is.

### No One Works on Their First Day

This is, in my experience, universally true. Sometimes there'll be one specific project you're given, but your first day is usually a strange mixture of overstimulation (here's your desk, there's the bathroom, talk to Josephine about computer privileges, please complete these forms, etc.) and unsettling lulls. In theory you should have a training session at some point, but onboarding takes work, and in a busy office you might have to amuse yourself for a while before they get around to making you a part of the team.

If you're a conscientious person, this is maddening, because you're there to *work* and you have no idea how to contribute. It's extra maddening if you're easily distractible because the entire Internet is just a few clicks away. You don't want to wander around the office pestering people into delegating tasks your way, but you also don't want to be blatantly perusing Facebook all day while you're still firmly within the first-impression stage. Regardless of your temperament, the remedy for channeling the nervous energy of an unstructured first day is the same: absorb as much information as you can while you await further instructions.

If you're given a formal training manual, read it cover-to-cover. If there's a fileshare that's relevant to the work you'll be doing, familiarize yourself with its contents (assuming you have permission to do so, obviously). Get your desk area organized and make a list of things you need (paper clips, sticky notes, etc.) for whenever you're given a chance to grab supplies. Set up your e-mail signature. Read the organization's website. Then, and only then, can you take a (short) break for online pleasure reading—ideally something tangentially work-related like the news, and only if no one's watching you. Even then, be prepared to abandon it at a moment's notice.

After you've truly exhausted your options for professional productivity, check back in with whoever's shamaning you through the new-hire process and ask (again) if there's anything you can do, or any meetings you can sit in on. If you strike out, ask if anyone else could use your help, and then go seek out those people. The goal here is to keep yourself busy—and demonstrate diligence—while waiting out the period when you're utterly inexperienced.

In every new job I've had, there've been a few days of feeling like a complete waste of space that suddenly give way into a complete sensation of I Totally Work Here. It's a natural transition and an entirely typical part of joining an office, so just trust that in time you'll feel less awkward, out-of-place, and useless.

### Making Acquaintances

The other time-honored First Day ritual is being introduced to your new coworkers. This will be a quick tour in a small office with the potential to be agonizingly long in a bigger one—and the more people you meet, the greater the likelihood that at least a few of them will react to your presence with a mixture of irritation and indifference. If (when) this happens, don't take it personally.

While *you* know that you're a vibrant human being full of insights, hopes, and dreams, to them you're just a name, a body, and a distraction from whatever they were in the middle of—and while you're coming from the perspective of "big debut at your new job," to them, it's just another busy workday. So let the personal connections happen when you both have the downtime to let them develop naturally.

### Lunch Break

You'll need nutritional fortification for all this meeting and learning, so during your first day/first week—the period before you develop a rhythm and set of habits—opt for whatever food-acquisition strategy seems like the path of least resistance.

If your office is in an urban area replete with walking-distance lunch options, then it's reasonable to assume that you'll have the chance to duck out and grab a sandwich/burrito/salad/whatever. But if there aren't any restaurants nearby, or if you're someone for whom "I could eat" rapidly escalates to "I am ravenous and angry," I'd suggest you BYO food so that you don't find yourself attempting to gnaw off your own hand during a training session. You might also want to bring a few shelf-stable snacks to stash in your desk for unexpected moments of hungritude.

First days are full of unknowns and the anxiety that accompanies a sense of uncertainty. The more mental energy you expend on tertiary things like "what will I eat and when," the less you'll be able to devote to things like "how to access the company intranet." So bring something you won't mind eating—and, while I'm sure the location of the communal fridge will be eventually revealed to you, something sufficiently cold-packed or otherwise immune to extended non-refrigeration—just in case other options don't present themselves. If you end up making plans to grab lunch with coworkers on your first day, great! That's two lunches taken care of. And if you learn you've been scheduled in back-to-back meetings and the nearest restaurant is a fifteen-minute drive away, you won't have to struggle through your afternoon weak from hunger.

**Learn by Doing**

Soon your first day will become your second day, and little by little you'll check all kinds of other first-time achievements off your list of workplace experiences. Even more senior people need to adapt to local customs once they start a new job, and unless you're working somewhere dysfunctional with a crappy culture, your coworkers are going to be more than willing to help you adjust. If you're curious about How Things Are Done, often the easiest route to enlightenment is just asking—your boss, someone else on your team, or the person (often the office manager) who seems to know everything.

The basic rule for your early days on the job is this: people will give you guidance, and as long as you demonstrate that you're able to take feedback, they'll forgive the minor missteps that accompany the learning process.

# Wardrobe Dysfunction

*Dress for the job you want and the job you have without blowing your entire paycheck*

Dear Businesslady,

I'm trying to make a good impression in a newish job, but I'm really struggling with something that seems ridiculously basic on its surface: actually dressing myself like a human being every day. I'm a recent grad and I feel like my wardrobe definitely skews in a direction you might call "college-y"— I've got cute/ironic/nerdy t-shirts for days, but if you want me to look "professional" apparently I just wear the same two pairs of dress pants with about six cheap button-downs that I don't even like.

The women I look up to in my office have a seemingly endless supply of effortlessly elegant outfits, but I have barely any disposable income for shopping unless I want to bust out my credit card, so I feel like I'm stuck until I get a raise. How do people develop work wardrobes when they're still at the entry level?

—The Other Day Someone Said
"You Wear That Shirt a Lot" and I Wanted to Die

➡ Oh, man, "work clothes"—the scourge of many postcollege wardrobes. One place's sharp outfit is another place's "why are you so dressed up" and yet another's "you're wearing *that?!*" Just show up on day one with your best guess of what "professional" looks like, and then go from there—*without* (I can't stress that enough) going into massive debt while trying to update your look for the workplace.

### Seriously, You Look Fine

I know that there are highly fashion-conscious offices out there, and I'm assuming that no one takes a job at *Vogue* believing that they can wear the same four Old Navy shirts for their entire tenure. I also know that there are ultra-casual workplaces where "anything that doesn't violate indecent exposure laws" is fair game. I see you, outliers, but this chapter is for everyone else—although the fashionistas and super-dressed-down might still find some valuable advice in what follows.

Even if you have a public-facing job—and especially if you don't—your appearance is not your most important contribution to the office. You are there to *work*, and as long as your physical presentation isn't actively hampering that, whatever you're wearing is probably fine. Yes, "fine" may not necessarily be the standard you're hoping to meet, but professional life is all about organizing your priorities. Most people are not going to be paying much attention to what you wear, and even if they happen to notice, they're unlikely to care. If they both notice and care, then they should be polite enough to keep their assessments to themselves, and if they can't manage *that*, well, I'd still argue that you shouldn't allow rude people to direct your dressing and shopping behaviors.

But, honestly, think back to the last time you were around a bunch of different people—at a restaurant, in a store, in an airport—and then think about how much time you spent assessing their fashion choices, or how well you can remember anyone's clothing in retrospect. You might notice the highly unusual or exceptionally stylish, but everyone else recedes into a general texture of "other humans, not nude." Use people's inherent self-absorption to your advantage and trust that no one is paying as much attention to your appearance as you are. I've gone on runs of wearing a favorite outfit with excessive frequency, and even my closest work friends have looked at me blankly when I pointed it out.

### The Cash You Save May Be Your Own

Now that we've established that your wardrobe isn't the biggest deal, I have a follow-up point: Do not go into debt by buying clothes (or, you know, anything else if you can avoid it). If you spend money you don't have trying to look as fancy as people with far bigger salaries, you will eventually have a much worse problem on your hands than "could maybe be more fashionable." It's amazingly easy to let a "just this once" splurge become a regular habit—something I learned the embarrassing, anxiety-inducing, debt-accruing hard way—and once your financial resources go negative, it's tough to turn things back around.

New clothes can seem like a worthy investment in your professional future, and in some cases you will in fact need to shell out some cash to enhance your wardrobe—I'm not trying to say that one $250 shopping trip is going to ruin you. Just be very careful about not spending more than you can afford, and choose your purchases wisely.

### Now, to the Shopatorium!

Okay, now we get to the fun part: shopping. (Even if you don't like shopping, I assume you enjoy it more than lectures about responsible budgeting.) In my early career, I definitely perceived a clear line between my "work clothes" and my "real clothes," and in most instances there was little overlap between them: weekends were for sundresses and ripped jeans, while the work week was for . . . frumpy stuff I hated wearing. But now—while I still dress differently for the office than I do for binging on video games— those categories have gotten a lot more porous. You spend an enormous proportion of your life at work, so you might as well spend it feeling (and looking) like yourself.

If you're trying to shift your wardrobe into a more professional direction, start by thinking about the commonalities between what you wear in "real life" and more office-appropriate outfits. Do you like bright colors or neutrals? Layers? Pants, or skirts, or dresses? When you admire the wardrobe of professionally dressed people of the same general demographic as yourself, what are they wearing? I wasted a lot of time and money buying ugly clothes just because they were suitable for work, and I want to spare you the same fate.

After you've figured out the kind of look you're going for, consider the pieces that are already in your closet and how they might interact with any new additions. For example, if you have a favorite cardigan + dress combo, then another cardigan and another dress—both of which coordinate with their predecessors—could instantly give you a few new outfits to play with. If you're someone who enjoys accessories, you can get more mileage out of your pricier clothes by using relatively inexpensive add-ons to create additional permutations.

Once you've established a budget and an aesthetic, then you hit the stores (or their websites). If you have a gift card or a generous benefactor, you might be able to reinvent your wardrobe in one fell swoop, but even then, be careful that you're not shopping aspirationally ("I'm not sure about this blazer, but if I got a new purse that matched . . ." or "I bet I could become someone who wears jumpsuits"). Don't buy anything you wouldn't wear, like, tomorrow. At the same time, if you run across an outfit that feels right to you—even if it's different from anything you've worn before—go for it. You're updating your style, which has the potential to prompt big changes, and there can be psychological power in treating yourself to something that feels special.

## Wearing It Well

Any other clothing suggestions would start wending too closely into the territory of individual fashion choices, which are too personal for me to try to art-direct from the other side of this page. The point is, buy things you like, that feel like "you," and that help breathe new life into the clothes you already own. Buy the highest quality stuff you can afford, but—say it with me now—don't spend beyond your means.

Remember that most people won't even notice what you're wearing unless it's something wildly inappropriate for the workplace. And if "wildly inappropriate for the workplace" is your look of choice, I've got some advice for you too.

# Wardrobe Assumptions

*Trying to look "normal" at work when
you're not a "normal"-looking person*

Dear Businesslady,

I'm having a hard time getting hired, and I think it's because of my appearance. I don't like to think of myself as a hipster (does anyone?) but I probably fit whatever image that conjures up: I have a septum piercing, gauges in my ears, full-sleeve tattoos (that I adore, and hate to imagine concealing!), and my hair is usually cut in an "edgy" style and dyed a fun color (right now, it's a mohawk in variegated shades of green, teal, and blue). I'm annoyed because I'm trying to use my graphic design degree and I feel like the way I look is a reflection of who I am: creative, visually oriented, and unique. I'm not applying to be the receptionist of a retirement home or something, so why do my looks even matter to employers?

Obviously I'm bitter about this, but working indefinitely at a coffee shop (where everyone loves my style but where I'm barely making enough for rent) isn't a viable long-term plan. Should I just grow out my hair and dye it back to its regular color (which is, I think . . . brown?), take out my piercings, and wear long sleeves for all eternity until I'm finally a desirable enough employee to be myself again? I guess that's one solution, but I wish I didn't have to pretend to be someone I'm not in order to get a job in my field.

—Aren't We Past This by Now?

→ It's true that norms are shifting in terms of what's considered "professionally" "appropriate" (with the quotes intended to reflect the breadth of both those terms). But it's also true that that most office-type jobs are going to have some ceiling on what they'll accept, whether that threshold is a piercing, a hairstyle, the size/placement/subject matter of a tattoo, or some other form of self-expression. So, where does that leave us?

## The Right to Tat and Bare Arms (Is Not an Actual Right)

Your right to look the way you want to look ends where your office's dress code begins—and really, that's no different from so many other aspects of working life. Being employed means giving up certain forms of autonomy.

Which is to say that *of course* having tattoos doesn't make you a worse graphic designer, just like blue-haired people can be great project managers, pierced-up people can be fantastic bookkeepers, and people who exclusively wear latex can be geniuses at developing marketing strategies. But nevertheless, the business world tends to adhere to certain standards for workplace attire and appearance—and whoever has the jobs makes the rules.

If I can step onto my soapbox for a sec, I'd like to point out that you don't *have* to dye your hair, get tattooed, or otherwise present yourself a certain way—which I say with full respect for the importance of feeling comfortable in one's own skin. We all exist in bodies that align (or don't) with society's concept of "normal" to varying degrees, and for many people that means facing discrimination no matter how hard they try to fit in. Being rejected from a job because you have a nose ring or blue hair isn't the same as being rejected because of other more inherent qualities, and while it would be great if *that* didn't happen either, we can't lump all those things together under one umbrella of "injustice." There is a difference between choosing to deviate from the norm and having that choice made for you. But practically speaking, if you're trying to get a professional job while choosing to rock an "unprofessional" look, you have a few basic options to choose from.

## Option #1: Have a Secret Identity

For the widest array of opportunities, you can keep your stylistic eccentricities under wraps from the interview onward. That may mean covering tattoos, removing piercings, or deploying wigs (either to hide funky-colored hair or as a way of re-creating it when you're off the clock). In time, you might be able to reincorporate the edgier aspects of your personal style. I wouldn't recommend suddenly showing up one day enrobed in body art with hot-pink hair, but if people in similar roles are getting away with [whatever], that's a safe bet that you can too, especially once you've proven that your work is solid.

## Option #2: Meet 'Em Halfway

To my knowledge there's no universally accepted gradient of piercings/tattoos/hairstyles, but common sense dictates that they're not all created equal—having a bunch of earrings is fine almost anywhere, whereas those cheek piercings that make it look like you have dimples are probably going to hold you back from a lot of office jobs. Even if your personal ideal is on the extreme side of "normal" (acknowledging that normalcy is both a social construct and a constantly moving target), you might be able to make small tweaks that help split the difference between typical office looks and your preferred appearance. So as a hypothetical, maybe you cover your neck tattoo with makeup during the workday, but leave your below-the-neck ink untouched.

The advantage to this versus the full-stealth option is that you're giving employers some indication of your stylistic unconventionalities which thus, presumably, will help you find a job at a place with a more relaxed dress code. And again, even if you start out more subdued, you might be able to evolve your look into something that feels more natural to you.

## Option #3: Make No Compromises

The third option, of course, is to hold firm and show up to every interview with your personal style choices on full display.

Some offices don't care about appearances one way or another (particularly if they're a work-from-home outfit where everyone just manifests as text on a screen anyway), and others cultivate a culture that favors the fashion-forward and edgy. If you're able to take your time with a job search and weed out the stuffier places, you should eventually find the right fit.

The only drawback to this approach is that many places aren't going to be able to deal with anything that constitutes a Look, so you'll likely endure a lengthier lead time before landing your new professional gig.

### Calculated Risks

In the end, my advice to the pierced/tattooed/unconventionally coiffed and their ilk depends on how desperately you need a job and what your personal comfort allows. By all means, start out with your style dialed up to 11, and then see how things go during your interviews. If you keep striking out—and especially if you notice eyes widening with dismay whenever you show up—then start toning it down to whatever extent you can handle. This is especially true the more junior you are. As you move forward in your career and become more of a specialized candidate, you'll be in a better position to dictate that your style and your sought-after skills are a package deal.

# Even If You Don't Write for a Living, You Write for a Living

*Effective workplace communication, including e-mail etiquette and tone*

Dear Businesslady,

Can we agree that it's stupid to get all worked up over typos and things like that in e-mail? I'm not new to the workforce so I know I'm not totally incompetent at communication, but I just started a new job where everyone is apparently a secret editor or something. It feels like every time I send out an e-mail, I get a response back about how it was too long, or too short, or how there was this typo, and it's making me not want to even try to communicate with anyone. The other day I e-mailed someone senior to me and didn't start out with "Dear So-and-so," and the recipient asked my boss to give me a talking-to! I don't get it. I'm not a writer, that's not what I'm paid for, so why is everyone obsessed with nitpicking my every word? If it's clear what I mean, does it really matter if there's the occasional "teh" or whatever?

—I Just Wanna Reply-All "SHUT UP!"

➡ your so rite idk why ppl care bout grammer bc as long as u can b understood then its like whatevs

HA HA, JUST KIDDING.

You may not care about the stuff you write at work, but you're doing yourself a disservice if you don't put some effort into it. Even when you see people face-to-face on a regular basis, their impressions of you will be shaped by the e-mails you send them—whether you like it or not. And as the workforce becomes increasingly hospitable to remote employees and increasingly reliant on written communication, you could be hampering your career prospects by displaying a flagrant disregard for textual accuracy and clarity.

## Okay But Like Why Tho

I know that everyone's busy and strapped for time and that if you're writing as quickly as possible that might mean you don't always make the best editorial choices. To a point, that's fine—for example, I think the preceding sentence should have at least one comma in it somewhere, but I'm guessing no one just threw this book across the room due to its insufficient punctuation. E-mail is indeed a casual medium, and if you're taking an hour to write a few short sentences, you're probably overthinking it.

However! The e-mails you send at work are an integral part of your professional identity. They become documents of your opinions, knowledge, and suggestions. While some are instantly disregarded after they're read (if they're read at all), others will be saved, referred to, looked up—even after you've moved on to a different job. They *persist*, and that means any errors or unnecessarily jumbled syntax remains inextricably linked to your colleagues' sense of Who You Are.

Again, I'm not saying that you should spend your whole morning weighing "Please feel free to contact me for more information" against "Don't hesitate to follow up if you need anything else," paralyzed with fear that you'll pick the wrong option. I also understand that people have different writing styles, and that I—someone who delights at the opportunity to edit things—have very different feelings about this than someone who hates to write. All I'm saying is: give things a quick proof before you hit Send (especially if the content goes beyond a simple "Okay, got it"). And if your managers offer constructive criticism about your e-mail voice, take it seriously.

### An E-Mail Is Not a Journal Entry

I'm clearly in the "likes writing" camp, and unlike a lot of my friends and coworkers I (usually) don't find e-mail-writing to be an arduous chore. But nevertheless, I've received some fairly incisive feedback about my approach to e-mails: namely, that they're way less concise than they ought to be. Some people take a "get it over with" approach that can risk coming off a bit terse or cold, but we writing types can have the opposite problem, reveling in the magic of combining words without sufficient attention to the desired result of the communication.

Or, maybe you're just stressed and strapped for time, and as a result you just free-write everything you have to say on a given topic—that happens too.

When writing e-mails, your focus should begin with the content you're trying to get across. If your boss asks for "everything you can find in our files about the Pembleton account," it's easy to interpret that literally and write a looooooong e-mail wherein minutiae is jumbled together with the most important details. After all, you don't know exactly what they're looking for, so why not be thorough, right?

Except, everyone with an e-mail account feels overwhelmed by the volume of messages they receive, and even taking the time to figure out "is this useful to me?" can feel like a huge hassle to a busy person.

So in the Pembleton example, I'd start with whatever seems like the most important takeaway from your findings. If you really feel like the remaining info is worth including, go ahead and lay it out, but only after you've addressed the big picture—that way if you've misjudged the level of specificity your boss needs, they can quickly skim the rest without worrying about missing something crucial.

You could also just wrap up after the highlight reel, saying something like "If you'd like more detail, I'd be happy to summarize the last few annual reports—and if you're looking for anything in particular, let me know."

After you've drafted an e-mail, read through it with your audience in mind. Is the information organized in a logical way, with the most significant points at the forefront—or have you written three paragraphs about the agenda for an event before finally getting around to the date and time it takes place? Is the subject line something descriptive like "New guidelines for expense reports" or something maddeningly vague like "Update"? The goal here is simplification and clarity: here's the topic, here's what you're saying about it, and done. Anyone who really wants to scroll past a bunch of aimless crap can go to their Twitter feed.

### Asked and Answered

Here's another pro tip from my time in the e-mail trenches. If you need a specific response—particularly from a manager or anyone senior to you—make sure that's explicitly stated at the outset. If you bury it at the end, then mark my words, you will receive "Wednesday" in response to a yes/no question, or else no reply at all, stalling a project while you await the recipient's input. Then you'll have to send *another* e-mail, wasting everyone's time in the process.

On a related note, avoid open-ended questions whenever possible (again, especially when e-mailing higher-ups instead of peers). Think about what a pain in the ass it can be to write an e-mail, and then picture the natural reaction to a message like "Here is a situation. What should we do?" versus "Here is a situation. Do you agree with the course of action I'm proposing?" The first response is gonna be a whole *thing*, whereas the second can be as simple as "Sure."

### Read the Room

When you join a new office, pay attention to the general style of the e-mails you receive. Are they casual/jokey/friendly? Or crisp/

succinct/polished? Do your colleagues open with a salutation, and if so, which one? "Dear," "Hello," and "Hi," while all within the realm of typical e-mail conventions, each suggests a slightly different vibe. After you've been in the workforce a while, it can be jarring to switch between workplaces with different e-mail philosophies, but if you adapt to the local culture, you won't offend your coworkers' sensibilities by seeming way too laid-back or way too formal.

You don't have to exactly mirror everyone else's writing, of course—but you'll want to temper your personal style against everyone else's. If you get feedback about doing things differently, listen to it. Yes, hearing something like "you use too many exclamation points" can feel petty, but if you ignore that warning it probably means your e-mails will become a source of irritation to the people who will eventually be considering you for promotions and raises. So . . . maybe not the hill you want to die on, you know?

## The Businesslady Manual of Style

- For your first e-mail to someone who's senior to you, use "Dear [Name]" unless that's Very Much Not Done in your workplace. If they respond with a friendlier greeting, you can follow suit, but it's better to seem overly deferential than presumptuous.
  - Use *some* kind of salutation for the initial e-mail in a new conversation, unless you're pretty close with whoever you're writing to. Omitting that opening "Hi" doesn't save enough time to balance out the potential consequences of seeming too brusque.
- While exclamation points can convey friendliness if deployed in reasonable quantities, they eventually reach a critical mass and become ridiculous. It's not an exact science, so be judicious (if you use them at all) and, again, follow your colleagues' lead. If you end every sentence with an exclamation, it will seem like you're shouting! Or otherwise unnervingly enthusiastic and chipper! And it feels weird to read! The same goes for multiple

question marks—they can work in small doses?? But they seem kinda unprofessional in aggregate, am I right????!?!?

- If you're inclined to use a smileyface to express "I'm joking" or "I'm being friendly," go ahead—as long as you do it sparingly. That means no more than once per message, and not in *every* message. If your jokes are so easily misconstrued without an accompanying icon, you might want to reconsider them altogether. No matter what you'd like to believe, smileyfaces aren't a magic spell that prevents any negative interpretation of the preceding text. Used too frequently, they start to grate—think of them like a nervous giggle, and then think about how you'd sound nervous-giggling after every single thing you said. You might not necessarily get told that you're overusing smileys (although I can say from experience that if you *are*, it's not the greatest feeling), but readers will be irritated by them regardless.

- Don't reply-all to listhost-type e-mails with a massive number of recipients—particularly if you don't know all of them personally. *Definitely* don't reply-all to bitch about how everyone else on the thread needs to stop hitting reply-all.

- Be very careful about bcc-ing people. (That's where someone receives your e-mail but the primary recipient can't see that they were copied, like a super-secret, hush-hush form of cc-ing.) It can occasionally be useful—like if your boss tells you "please let me know if you have to keep bugging Larry for those reports" so you bcc your boss on your umpteenth e-mail to Larry—but it can also be dangerous. The bcc-ed person could potentially reply-all to the e-mail you sent, which means that if you were trying to be stealthy the gig is up.

- Be equally careful about cc-ing people—if you're trying to shame a coworker into action by cc-ing their boss, that's a pretty dick move. In addition to being adversarial, it's also likely to annoy the boss (even if they might've otherwise been sympathetic to your plight) because they now need to wade through the e-mail thread to figure out why you copied them. If your colleague isn't doing their job, there are better ways of addressing that. (For more on horse-whispering your more difficult colleagues into doing your bidding, see Chapter 5.) The boss-cc approach is simultaneously aggressive and lazy.

- Finally, while Microsoft Outlook provides a red exclamation-point button for marking e-mails "urgent," think long and hard about what "urgent" actually means before using it. For something truly immediate like "That meeting that starts in thirty minutes has just been canceled"—fine, I'll allow it. But if you use it to say "Hey guys, I think this e-mail is important!" then I will be very disappointed in you.

And since Outlook is the most common program for office e-mail, here are two more software-specific tidbits: If you forward a calendar invitation, your accompanying commentary will be shared with the original sender (so "wanna come to this dumb meeting?" is gonna get you into trouble). And if you see a message with an inexplicable "J" at the end, that's a smileyface that got converted weirdly in the digital ether.

### I Have a Calling

This section is mainly about e-mail because apparently no one wants to use the telephone anymore unless it's for texting. But believe it or not, phones are still frequently used for communication in a lot of offices—including, but not limited to, situations where you don't want to risk incriminating yourself by putting something in writing.

I realize that the immediacy of the phone can be stressful, and I understand why keeping things textual can seem like an easy workaround. But since e-mail creates a paper trail, you'll often get more useful and nuanced info via a more ephemeral medium. If you're trying to cajole a favor out of someone, begin the process of untangling a screwup, get the inside scoop on something theoretically confidential, or communicate a delicate message where tone is vital, consider giving your typin' fingers a break and picking up a handset for some good-ol'-fashioned human-to-human talking.

## You Have One New Message

If you're up to the challenge of the occasional phone conversation, you'll periodically have to leave voicemails—your appearance on someone's caller ID isn't enough to make them call you back. When leaving a message, it's easy to fall into the same info-dump trap that plagues novice e-mailers, only it's even worse because the listener has no way to skim. So don't use voicemail to convey information beyond "I called you, now here's how to reach me" unless it's something very specific and uncomplicated. "The deadline for the catalogs is Wednesday" is fine. "I was wondering if maybe we should try to get the catalogs out sooner because Terrance is going on vacation at the end of next week and if we wait until he gets back then they might not ship in time for our usual holiday orders" is not. (See how exhausting that was to read? Now imagine hearing someone ramble it into your ear.)

Unless you've called someone you know well and talk to frequently, your voicemail should include your name, your reason for calling, your phone number—and then repeat it since people often need a second to grab a pen. (Yes, almost everyone has caller ID these days, but that doesn't mean everyone wants to wade through the deep menu hierarchy on their overcomplicated office phone in order to find your particular missed call.) Plus, voicemail systems are apparently designed to make it a pain in the ass to rewind, so err on the side of repetition. Here's a template: "Hi, this is Businesslady, calling from the Bookatorium. I just wanted to talk with you about leaving good voicemails, so please give me a call back at 555-555-5555. Again, that number is 555-555-5555 and this is Businesslady from the book you're currently reading. I'll look forward to talking with you soon." You can throw in practical details like "I'll be available until 3 P.M. and then all day tomorrow" if you want, but save the rest of the content for the actual conversation.

Or, *fine*, send an e-mail instead.

# #NotSafeForWork

*Maintaining an appropriate online presence*

Dear Businesslady,

I need some guidelines for what I'm allowed to put up on social media now that I've got a desk job. I'm not an idiot, I know that I shouldn't document drug use or excessive drinking or a time-stamped photo of myself at a baseball game on a day I was "out sick." But what about political debates on Twitter? Or friending my coworkers on Facebook? Or the occasional risqué selfie on my Tumblr (which is under a pseudonym btw)?

It feels like there's no middle ground between "you're an adult, do what you want" and ABSOLUTE TOTAL DISCRETION—my parents act like I'll get fired if someone tags me in a picture where I'm holding a beer, but then some of my friends' public Instagram feeds are unabashedly full of weed paraphernalia (and to my knowledge, none of them have lost their jobs over it . . . yet).

I don't want to ruin my career over some stupid post, but I also don't want to keep myself on unnecessary lockdown out of sheer paranoia. Is there an actual middle ground here after all?

—Set to Private

→ Before I answer this, let's just all imagine what it was like to live in an era where the odds of anyone you worked with discovering your sordid extracurricular activities were slim to none. Unless you physically *ran into* a coworker while out and about, or your presence ended up getting noted in the news for some reason, the worst thing you had to deal with was gossip—which is well known to be unreliable.

Of course, those days are long gone. Now, even if you're rigorous about your own privacy controls, you still have the possibility of friends or acquaintances with freely visible pages tagging you in photos you'd rather not release to the world. Plus, with various social media sites increasingly linking up with one another, you might not even realize that your coworkers are privy to your Yelp reviews of local sex-toy purveyors (or whatever other conflation of your public and private life keeps you up at night).

You know what, though? It's going to be fine. Probably. Here's how to avoid getting screwed by your online presence.

### Know Your Role

Certain jobs have more rigorous standards than others in terms of Internet-related behavior. If you're in a position where an ill-considered post could potentially go viral (a teacher, say, or the employee of a prominent public figure), then you probably have to be more cautious than the rest of us. And even if you're not in a high-profile industry, you should be mindful of the kinds of scenarios that are like catnip for the online outrage machine. If you're talking shit about people who are part of your professional circle, or about companies that are competitors or collaborators, that's much more likely to draw negative attention than a rant about how someone was rude to you at the local deli.

### Common Sense

Even if your privacy settings are designed to prevent unfriendly eyes from seeing your stuff, don't assume that's bulletproof. It's unlikely that your boss and coworkers are constantly scouring the Internet to see if you've posted something controversial, but you never know what might somehow get noticed. So if there's a photo/opinion/story/whatever that you wouldn't want them seeing . . . don't post it.

I know, that's no fun. But isn't being gainfully employed more important than showing everyone on Tumblr your cool new bong?

If you simply must share every detail of your life, regardless of its work-appropriateness, don't post the racier stuff in a venue that's linked to your real name and identity. Even an anonymous or pseudonymous account could be eventually traced back to you, but the more digging people have to do, the less likely it is that you'll be held accountable (and even if someone does do the requisite investigation, you can at least point out that you were trying to distance yourself from the objectionable content).

## Love Me, Love My Feed

Of course, there's a huge grey area between "illegal or provocative behavior" and "completely boring update about your laundry routine," and if you're an avid social media user it's hard to say where the line should be drawn in terms of what you post. Part of the problem with freely available online content is that anyone could potentially see *anything*, and what you consider a benign comment could read to someone else as #ShotsFired. That's not necessarily a workplace problem, but if colleagues or managers become part of the fray, it could be. Additionally, it's safe to assume that if you're on the job market, your potential employer will do some searching to see if there are any skeletons hiding in your Internet closet.

In other words, online posting carries a certain risk—you have to accept that someone, somewhere, might punish you for anything you do. If you've applied for a position where your would-be manager is an avid animal-rights activist, and she runs across your Instagram photo of a sweet new fur coat—well, you probably won't get that job. But arguably your fur-loving self and Ms. PETA wouldn't have been a good match anyway, and the same holds true for being outspoken about political views or anything else that's important to you—it helps weed out less like-minded people. If you're willing to take that gamble, then go forth and share widely with the world. Just: eyes open, my friend.

## A Sense of Proportion

Your Internet presence also goes beyond any one individual post—it's ultimately about the overall image that you present. If you have a typically jokey, conversational Twitter feed with one single tweet where you mock Taylor Swift, that's going to read very differently than an account filled with nonstop celebrity harassment. Similarly, the occasional partytime photo is different than hundreds of pictures where you're clutching a booze vessel for dear life and seem like you're seconds away from passing out.

If you want to post liberally in venues that overlap with your professional circle, try to think about the big picture you're putting out there. You might consider setting up an official webpage that emphasizes your workly self, pin a job-appropriate tweet to your Twitter profile, and/or make sure you're on LinkedIn even if you spend (way) less time there than you do on Facebook.

## The Friendening

Speaking of Facebook . . . invite coworkers into your online/real life at your discretion, knowing that it can be dicey territory. It's tough to accept some people's friend (or follow) requests and not others—someone might let it slip that certain folks didn't make the cut. Then there are situations that put you in a real bind, like if you want to post about something without anyone at work finding out about it (like a sick day that turned into an impromptu picnic, or a new job offer when you haven't resigned from your old job yet . . . or, you know, bitching about your coworkers themselves).

Being Facebook friends with work people is fine, but you'll do yourself a favor by putting them in a separate category so that—on the occasions where it's necessary—you can exclude them from any particular post with a few taps. There are settings that make it easy, and they'll never have to know that you've put them in a different class from everyone else who populates your feed.

The other potential downside to friending coworkers is that you might learn things about *them* that you wish you could unlearn, but that's the cost of getting to know other people, I suppose.

## Deletion Is Always an Option

Ideally, your Internet presence and your career will remain in separate spheres, unless you're in an industry where they're inextricably linked or you otherwise have a reason to merge them. If you start feeling worried about your past posts, or want to start networking via Twitter without drawing eyes to some questionable content, don't forget that you can undo the past to some extent.

Sure, the Internet is technically forever, and there's always some slim chance that your embarrassing blog from high school is going to resurface even though you're *sure* you took it down. But the more sleuthing people have to do to find dirt on you, the less likely it is that they'll bother. Plus, if they do resurrect something shameful from your deep history, people will be more sympathetic if you clearly tried to delete it. So periodically review your public Internet archives and remove/hide/privatize anything that seems like a bad idea in retrospect.

# "Awake and Alert" Is Non-Negotiable

*The care and feeding of your job-having self*

Dear Businesslady,

I was lucky enough to land a job I'm excited about right after graduation, and so far the work itself is going great—I get along well with my coworkers, I like and admire my boss, and I'm learning a lot while (I hope!) contributing to a company I'd like to stick with for the long term. I mean, I still have stressful days sometimes, but on the whole I know I've got it good compared to a lot of my friends.

Here comes the inevitable "but" . . . I feel like I might not be cut out for a 9-to-5 (or 8:30-to-5 in my case but you get the point). I am EXHAUSTED every morning, and once I even overslept—I somehow turned off my three(!) alarms while unconscious and it was only when my boss called me at 11:30 A.M., worried that I'd gotten hit by a bus or something, that I finally rejoined the living. (To say that was mortifying was an understatement and I'm just glad it wasn't on a day when it could've caused real problems.)

It makes no sense because I'm getting about as much sleep as I used to, on average—I stay up until midnight or so on weeknights (it's hard to fall asleep earlier!) and then I get up around 5:30 A.M. I know that doesn't sound like much, but I used to routinely get by on less than four hours of sleep in college, and then catch up on the weekends/whenever I could (which I'm doing now).

I don't know if I'm just uniquely weird in being unable to get it together, or if adults are all just exhausted all the time and that's something no one tells you when you're younger.

—Do People Really Get Up Before Noon on Saturdays?
(And *like* it?)

➡ Oh, I wish I could tell you that you're experiencing some kind of weird slump and that you'll soon regain your superhuman ability to function on little or no sleep. Alas, this is a book of real-world advice, not beautiful lies, and so I must be honest: this isn't going away, and in fact it only gets worse as you get older. But fear not! If you embrace the human body's need for rest and other forms of restorative sustenance, you can come to accept and even enjoy this new reality. There's nothing worse than encountering a workday crisis when your mental faculties are running on auxiliary power.

## Retrain Your Routine

First, believe me when I say I feel your pain. I come from a long line of night owls, and I thought I was destined to be infuriated by my alarm clock for the rest of my life. For at least a year after starting my first full-time office job, I rarely woke up before 2 P.M. on Saturdays and Sundays. Yet I always felt like I needed more sleep.

Leaving aside the fact that you can't really "catch up" on sleep in a meaningful way, you know what sucks about sleeping 'til 2 P.M.? It means that in the winter, it's already getting dark by the time you've gotten ready to go anywhere. It also means you're always scrambling to get to restaurants before their brunch menu ends. Most importantly, it means that you need to stay up until at least 3 A.M. to feel like you've really gotten to enjoy a full day's worth of weekending, and thus you restart the whole cycle over again. You're going into sleep debt, essentially, and replicating the work week's "can't do anything fun for most of the day" schedule during your supposedly free time.

If you manage to get up early on a Saturday, though? You have the *whole day to yourself*. You get to do whatever you want, in the daylight, for hours and hours.

I'm not saying I'm immune to the allure of a comfy bed on a lazy morning or that I don't occasionally find myself ill-advisedly trawling Wikipedia on a weeknight when I should be ensconced in slumber. But for the most part, I have managed to bring my work-necessitated waking hours into alignment with my own natural sleep cycle. I don't usually set alarms on the weekends, but it's rare that I sleep past 10 A.M., and I've been known to burst awake at 7:45 ready to start having fun.

I know that sounds unrealistic and unlikely, because I used to think the same thing—that I would never be able to establish a "normal" sleep routine. Except I did! If I could make it happen, then chances are you can too.

If you're sick of battling against the alarm clock whenever you have to wake up for work, retrain your body to the new normal. Set alarms on weekends as early as you can stand it, and start getting ready for bed earlier than you normally would. Make an effort to avoid late-night eating or afternoon caffeine or anything else that might undermine your attempts to fall asleep at a reasonable hour.

It's not going to happen instantly and you'll probably feel tired for a while as you readjust. But if you persevere, you'll eventually be getting enough sleep—and that means that when you want to stay up super-late every once in a while, your body will be fortified enough to handle it.

### Food for Thought on Food

As you can tell from my thoughts on sleep, this section—like a lot of the advice in this book—is inspired by Things I Learned the Hard Way. I struggled for a while to bring my sleeping habits in line with what my body (apparently) needed, and the same is true for my eating habits too.

I know that relationships with food are very personal, so I'm not trying to give diet tips or shame anyone's choices. But if you're accustomed to an eating routine of random grazing and occasional binges whenever free food presented itself (i.e., college), transitioning to the structured routine of a typical workday can be challenging. On a basic level, food and sleep are fuel for the body and mind, and as your bodily/mental activities change, your fuel inputs need to change too.

Or, more simply put: you're not going to do your best work if you're hungry—and, on the flip side, you're going to feel hungrier more often if you're consistently sleep-deprived.

So, make sure you're feeding yourself with whatever keeps your system humming along. Breakfast can happen at the office or before you get there (and even if you're a rebel who scoffs at popular wisdom regarding the most important meal of the day—I'm not big on it either unless we're talking brunch—I'd still recommend a bite or two of something with calories just to wake up your metabolism).

Lunch can be brought from home or bought, just so long as it's a regular part of your day—there's nothing worse than realizing at 3 P.M. that you're weak from hunger, and your only options are vending-machine foraging or venturing out in a snowstorm.

Ditto for dinner—do whatever you want, but make sure you're eating *something* at a reasonable evening hour, not just chowing whatever's on hand at 9 P.M. when you feel like you're starving to death. Nothing undermines the illusion that you're a competent adult like making a meal out of a handful of cookies and a doggie bag of soggy fries (and nutritionally there are some drawbacks to that combo too).

For bonus points, learning to cook can help you save money, plus it gives you a wider variety of sustenance options to choose from when you're staring into your fridge and cabinets. You don't have to become Cheffy McVegetables overnight—keeping yourself well fed at regular intervals is a good first step.

### Escape the Chair

One of the best things about eating during the workday is that it gives you a chance to escape your desk (even if you're just venturing to the office kitchen). Lunch only happens once, though, so don't forget that you're allowed to get up and move around without a specific destination.

If you're feeling stuck, if your eyes start glazing over, if you're getting irrationally irritated about something (and it's not because you're overdue for a meal), that's probably a sign that you need to walk around. Get outside if "outside" is easily accessible and the weather is nice, or wander over to the water cooler even if you're not really thirsty, or go say hi to someone you haven't chatted with for a while. (And if you feel like you need coffee but it's too late in the day for caffeine, trick yourself into wakefulness with a cup of decaf. That's a lifehack I recently discovered, and it's amazing.) Just do *something*, and you'll reset your body and brain.

This is especially crucial if you're feeling overworked and pressed for time, because it's easy to delude yourself into thinking that it's impossible for you to break your focus. But once you've hit a slump, your focus is *already* broken, so you might as well embrace it and try to overcome it. Treating yourself to the small luxury of a break will ultimately make you more productive. (And if you're really stressed, I've got some advanced-level techniques in Chapter 7.)

### Okay, Mom

Listen, I realize all this might seem silly, or patronizing, or (if you already have pretty well-structured habits) unnecessary. Still, even now, when I technically know better, I sometimes have to remind myself to respect my body's basic needs: to drink enough water, to go to bed on time, to eat something when it feels like my brain is shutting down. So I'm just trying to spare you the exhaustion and malnutrition that characterized my early career.

## CHAPTER 3

## GREAT, EXPECTATIONS:
# Settling Into Your Role When You're No Longer New

BEING NEW TO a job is a kind of protected status. There are so many things you can't possibly know yet, and therefore anything you manage to accomplish feels like a triumph over adversity: You remembered the code for the copier! You didn't get lost on the way back from the bathroom! You actually helped a coworker do a thing! Look at you, a paragon of professional success.

After a while, that new-employee gleam starts to wear off, and you become the version of yourself that you'll be until you switch jobs again. People stop checking in on how you're doing and start expecting you to handle your workload with minimal intervention. And if you're having trouble getting the hang of things, "I'm new here" is no longer a viable explanation.

Although it means you're shouldering more responsibilities, becoming more established in your workplace has its benefits too. When you're brand new, you're trying to prove yourself and build new relationships—both of which can make it tough to advocate for your own best interests and push back against people who are causing problems for you. That's not as much of a concern once you've become a known quantity. Given enough time, you can begin redefining the contours of your position—highlighting what you have to offer, adding new tasks to your purview, and realigning the things that aren't going well.

Even though your official training/onboarding period has an end point, your capacity to learn and grow continues indefinitely. Regardless of how long you've been in the same position, there are always ways to become more efficient, to make your contributions more visible, or to nudge your role in directions that increase your personal satisfaction.

You've already found a job and convinced them to hire you—after clearing those hurdles, the regular life of a worker bee can seem anticlimactic. Here's how to prevent inertia from setting in and keep yourself moving forward.

# How to Career, Part II

*Understanding and meeting your manager's expectations*

Dear Businesslady,

My boss is fantastic, but also super busy. Since I'm pretty low in the office hierarchy, she doesn't have a lot of time for one-on-one meetings with me, let alone mentorship. And I get it! I'm not some special entitled snowflake who needs a gold star for managing to get to a meeting on time. But am I totally wrong for wanting some validation, some kind of occasional "hey, keep up the good work" from my manager? I feel like the only interactions I have with her are about direct assignments, times when I'm stalking her trying to get an answer to a question, and then (the worst) Serious Conversations about things that didn't go as well as they could.

I'm not worried about job security per se—this company is notorious for cutting dead weight and I've been here over a year, so I know I'm not actively awful. I'd just like more guidance on how I'm doing, how I could be better, etc., without making unreasonable demands on my manager's limited time.

—Participation Trophy

➤ This is a common problem in a lot of workplaces: most bosses have a ton of things on their plate beyond "actively manage employees," and it can be easy to let that duty slide in the face of more pressing priorities. Paradoxically, the most hardworking and proactive people—the ones who have the most to gain from one-on-one mentorship and regular meetings—are often the ones who get the least attention.

Obviously that doesn't mean you should start actively making mistakes in the hope that you'll get noticed. Instead, you can make the most of your brief contact with a busy boss, and keep yourself feeling confident even when you've gone awhile without positive feedback.

### Getting on the Calendar

You don't want your boss to be some elusive figure you have to trek through misty jungles and up mountains to reach—so plan a regular meeting. Knowing "well, if nothing else, we'll talk on Thursday" will help counteract against the sense that they're in an entirely different universe. And although your manager's calendar might be packed to the gills, it will benefit them to have some dedicated time set aside to talk with you: instead of replying to five different e-mails and getting interrupted for three unrelated questions, you can save all the non-urgent stuff for your regularly scheduled conversation and run through it all at once.

You may not succeed, but do what you can to institute some habitual one-on-one time with your manager. If they're initially resistant, emphasize the ways it could make their life easier: "I feel bad interrupting you with one-off questions and updates—I know you're really busy, but is there any way you could carve out a half-hour a week for us to talk? If we don't need the full time I'll be happy to cut it short, and you can always cancel if you're really swamped." While that still might not convince them, it'll get your point across that This Is Something I Want, and you can continue bringing it up until you decide it's truly futile.

## Let's Meet a While

Even the most employee-focused boss is sometimes going to have to cancel on you due to a crisis, but your manager will likely agree to a regular meeting of some kind. In general, you should shoot for around once a week (no more than that unless there's something big you need to keep meeting about), at least two or three times a month, and on some kind of predictable schedule.

While you can't spend these conversations fishing for compliments per se, you can get a sense of how you're doing by actively soliciting feedback. That means going beyond a simple rundown of your to-do list and the status of completed and ongoing projects. If you're not sure about how to handle something, or you're curious about your manager's take on something you already did, *ask*. And be prepared to listen attentively to the answer, even (especially) if it's anything other than "great job." If you want mentorship, then you have to understand constructive criticism is a major part of it—and if that's a challenge for you, then check out this chapter's section on feedback and see if it helps.

Most people don't just dispense wisdom via unprompted monologues (the format of this book notwithstanding). Instead, you'll learn from your boss's experience as they coach you on what you could be doing better or differently.

You can also judiciously mention some of your own points of personal pride during these meetings—"by the way, [boss's boss] was really happy with that report," etc. (and if that feels too self-promoting, you can spin it with a follow-up like "so thanks for helping me figure out how to organize it"). Don't be shy about sharing positive comments—it's stuff your boss might not hear about otherwise, and you want them to have the highest possible opinion of your work.

Even if you give up on setting official meetings with your manager, you might be able to create a stealth meeting that exploits some recurrent downtime in their schedule—like maybe they're usually at their desk during lunch or always the first to arrive on Thursdays. Seize those moments to drop by and kick off an ostensibly spontaneous conversation. Unless they seem actively annoyed to see you, then hey: meeting achieved.

## Be Your Own Cheering Section

Depending on your manager's personality, workload, and over-all approach to leadership, you might not get feedback or face-time with regular frequency. And even if you do establish a meeting schedule, your boss probably won't spend that time bestowing accolades—after all, doing your job *well* isn't actually that different from simply doing your job, and that doesn't merit showers of praise.

Now, I'm not saying that expressing appreciation isn't impor-tant. As a manager, it's smart to make sure your highest performers feel valued. But this is advice for *you*, the lowly underling, and I can't make your boss give you the recognition you deserve. Any-one who's ever successfully wheedled out a compliment knows that it feels a lot less meaningful when it's not voluntarily given. In the end, you don't really need your employer's praise so much as you need more tangible rewards—like raises and promotions.

So if you're one of the many, many people with a too-busy boss who's bad about expressing gratitude for a job well done, start expressing it to yourself. Keep a file where you save the nice things that have been said about you by coworkers and clients, and supplement it with a list of things you're especially proud of. You might not ever hear "if you hadn't worked those ten-hour days, we would've missed that deadline," but you can know in your heart that it's true.

This isn't just about maintaining a healthy sense of self-esteem (although it's about that too). It's also about having a stockpile of ammunition ready when you have an opportunity to self-advocate: for more money, a better title, and/or responsibilities that are more in line with your long-term career goals. (See Chapter 7 whenever you're ready to put this into practice.)

## Zoom Out Periodically

It's not practical to be constantly hounding your boss for a comprehensive assessment of your performance, but all the same, you don't need to wait for your annual review to get their take on things. At regular intervals—on occasions when you know your boss isn't terribly pressed for time—you can ask for a more overarching critique. If there are particular things you're worried about, you can bring them up directly: "I feel like I still sometimes struggle with the supply-requisition process. Am I still within the typical learning curve there or should I be worried?" You can even request meta-feedback about the meetings themselves: "Should these updates be more detailed, or less, or would you rather I give a different slant on the info I'm sharing?"

Questions like this might successfully shake loose the occasional "you're doing great," which is always nice to hear. But even if the response is less enthusiastic, that knowledge will still benefit you in the long run. If you can feel confident that you're doing a better-than-merely-okay job, that will help you feel comfortable pushing back when you're asked to step your game up to superhuman levels.

# You're Only One Person

*Developing the skill of saying "no" and pushing back against unreasonable demands*

Dear Businesslady,

I fell into a really great position due to the collision of a temp gig, a sudden employee departure, and an office so under-staffed that they essentially had no choice but to trust me with important tasks. I've developed a reputation as a "fixer"—whenever anything needs doing and it's not obviously some-one else's job, it falls to me. And to be honest, I kind of love it. The sense of being needed, the excitement of not knowing what I'll be working on from day to day, the high-energy urgency—that stuff is all great.

But what's not great is when I'm already frantically trying to make magic happen for three different projects and some-one comes to me with a fourth. Or a fifth. Or it's the one night in three straight months that I've had the audacity to make plans right after work, and someone hands me a crisis at 4:58 P.M. Then I just feel overwhelmed and want to burst into tears like a toddler who just unexpectedly fell down.

People say "police your own time" but my role is so defined by my willingness to go above and beyond that I'm afraid of sending the message that I'm no longer the go-to person for these tasks that I genuinely enjoy (or at least appre-ciate the challenge of) 99% of the time. How can I tell people "no" and still get asked for help in the future?

—Gal Monday Tuesday Wednesday Thursday Friday
(and Sometimes Saturday & Sunday)

➤ This is probably the most important thing I have to say on the subject of being a human being with a job:

No one will ever tell you that you're working too much, too hard, or too well.

*Ever.*

I mean, sure, there might be moments when your boss stops by your desk at 6:30 and asks, "You're heading home eventually, right?" in a friendly and concerned tone. But in the grand scheme of things, you won't hear anyone say that you need to be easier on yourself. No one. Never. That's a message that can only come from within, and you'll never be able to say no to other people if you can't even say it to your own reflection.

### In Case You're Just Skimming the Headers: No One Will Ever Tell You to Dial Back Your Productivity

And if someone hasn't asked you to defy the laws of physics in the service of company deadlines, then you probably haven't been in the workforce very long. (Or else maybe you just have a naturally healthy set of boundaries and people can sense that about you, in which case congratulations and please tell me your secrets.)

### Bust Your Ass at Your Own Discretion

While the issue of protecting your time is a universal problem, it's also one that can be especially tricky when you're earlyish in your career because you're understandably focused on proving yourself. Being the standout person in a junior role is how you get promoted into a more senior spot, and going above and beyond your job description is how you demonstrate your ability to take on more complicated tasks. So I don't want to say that you need to push back just on principle. There are circumstances where you might do a cost/benefit analysis and decide that working yourself to the limit is ultimately in your own best interest—for example, if you're:

- About to see a massive project through to completion,
- In contention for a hugely meaningful promotion,
- Bouncing back from a royal screwup (more on that in a bit), or

- Trying to make a name for yourself in a highly competitive field.

That is absolutely your call to make.
However. *How-ev-er.*

## Bust Your Ass at Your Own Risk

The reason no one will ever tell you to take it down a notch is that no one else is as invested in your well-being as you are. Even the kindest, most empathetic, most genuinely supportive boss in the world is going to prioritize Getting Shit Done over worrying about employees' burnout. Meanwhile, less considerate managers are going to be truly indifferent to the toll your workload is taking.

It's easy to say yes to a major imposition "just this once," and when it ends up being twice, well, that's so close to once that you may not feel justified in objecting. You're not some slacker who leaves at 5:01 when everyone else is pulling all-nighters—you're a team player! Except that after you've established a precedent of "you can ask the unreasonable of me and I won't question it," it takes an even greater effort to draw boundaries.

To some extent, this is just the price of being accommodating: people will come to expect it, and then you have to deal with their disappointment when the only alternative is losing your mind from stress. Still, that doesn't mean that every time you say "yes," you have to do it with an attitude of unadulterated cheerfulness.

## Let It Be Known That Your Ass Is Being Busted

You don't want to respond to requests with a laundry list of reasons it's inconvenient for you to comply, but if people are genuinely imposing on you, you can make them aware of that in a polite way. Before you automatically cancel your dinner plans, blow a competing deadline, or resign yourself to working all weekend, make sure whatever-it-is actually warrants that level of effort. Even if your boss is the one doing the asking.

Unless your entire office is staffed by draconian assholes who actively want to spite you, most people are going to be sympathetic if you're feeling overwhelmed. Save the "no problem"s for when it really is no problem. Otherwise, try responses like "I *can* [do that thing] by the end of the day, but I'm supposed to get together with a friend after work—can it wait until tomorrow?" If the person you're talking to is your boss, you can make it clear that you'll have to reshuffle your priorities to accommodate them and see if it's really worth it from their perspective.

Sometimes, you'll be told that it has to get done no matter what, and that's when you suck it up (while simultaneously making a mental note of this instance when you put the organization's needs above your own). But often the timeline isn't actually that tight, or the person making the request would rather save their imposing-on-you capital for a more important project.

When you introduce this kind of "if you really need me to" caveat, you don't want to sound put-upon. The ideal tone is one of regret and concern, of "I hate to break it to you but this is a challenging situation"—the way you'd respond if someone just told you they needed to catch a flight in an hour and they're nowhere near the airport.

### Un-Busting Your Ass

After you get used to adding qualifications to your yesses, saying "no" will start to come more naturally. Once you finally turn someone down outright—"I'm sorry, I really can't, my brain will explode if I try to do one more thing before the end of the month"—you'll realize that you haven't permanently undermined your reputation. By contrast, if you try to take on too much, there will be consequences: you'll miss a deadline, you'll make a sloppy mistake because you're working too quickly, or you'll forget about the umpteenth thing you promised to help with. That stuff will do far more damage to your reputation than regretfully declining additional work. If you try these techniques and are still constantly fighting back claims on your time, you can enlist your boss as an ally—"I'm sorry, [manager] said I'm not allowed to embark on any new projects until this is finished." Similarly, if you're asked for a new favor while you're already doing a favor for someone else, you can "blame" that person for your insurmountable busyness—it proves that you take your commitments seriously and that you're realistic about your own capabilities. And if your boss is assigning you work faster than you can keep up with it, have a heart-to-heart about the demands of the job and whether or not they're reasonable. (I'll delve deeper into those kinds of potentially tough conversations in Chapter 6. Or if the problem isn't actually workload but your underdeveloped time-management skills, Chapter 4 has some suggestions.)

Protecting your time isn't always easy—in fact, it's frequently outright difficult, and its side effects could include guilt, frustration, and worry. But it's always better than the alternative.

You don't want to saddle yourself with an unsustainably high workload, and the only person who can prevent that is you.

# Surprising Yourself

## Tackling new challenges and adjusting to new responsibilities

Dear Businesslady,

I just got a huuuuge promotion and I'm suuuuuper excited—but also terrified. I've spent a long time agitating for a role with more responsibilities, but now it's a "be careful what you wish for" situation. I used to be just a person who does things but now I'm the person who decides what things should be done, and that level of control is overwhelming. I keep telling myself that I know what I'm doing, that I deserve this, that I wouldn't be in this position if I wasn't qualified—but in practice, I'm not sure how to seem like an authority when I technically have no idea what I'm doing. Is there a secret formula for finding the right balance between "Help, explain this to me!" and "I was born to do this"? Or am I just going to feel lost for a while?

—A Title Without a Story

➤ This problem is kind of like a cousin of impostor syndrome, where you erroneously feel unworthy of your own success. Except in your case, it's pretty reasonable for you to feel uneasy about your new position, because you're essentially learning to swim while you're already in the pool.

There are really two things you need to work on here: feeling confident about tackling the responsibilities that have just been handed to you, and strategically developing your skills so that you stop feeling like such a novice. Neither one is as difficult as you might think.

### You've Got This

Remember how I said no one works on the first day of a new job? The same is true with internal moves: no one's expecting you to be an instant expert at your new position. Plus, if you're promoted from within, that's based on hard data about your previous performance—presumably the decision-makers involved aren't in the habit of randomly rewarding unqualified people just to see what happens.

All of which is to say, if the higher-ups at your organization believe that you're capable of doing a certain kind of work, you should believe it too. They've had the opportunity to see you in action, and if they've completely misjudged your fit for the role, that's not your fault—it's theirs. So trust them, and more importantly, trust yourself.

### Smart People Ask "Stupid" Questions

As you're getting up to speed, you're going to have to educate yourself about the requirements of the new position—first the basic, practical aspects and then the more sophisticated, nuanced stuff that comes from experience. The best way to start accruing that knowledge is by picking the brains of whatever industry veterans you have access to—which if nothing else should include your more senior colleagues.

When you're attempting to level up professionally, your first impulse might be to fake it 'til you make it—and sure, I agree that you don't want to actively broadcast your confusion or inexperience. Playing the role of a seasoned expert will only get you so far, though, and it can really backfire if you prioritize optics over information-gathering. Have you ever known someone who tries to pretend they're never wrong? Someone who never asks questions, and who, when their ill-considered forging ahead causes problems, comes up with some excuse about how they knew what they were doing all along? Someone who is so afraid of being judged for acknowledging their imperfections that they never take steps to do better?

I think we all know that person. And I think we can all agree that person is *frustrating*.

It takes guts to pipe up in a meeting and say "You guys, I don't know what that acronym means—can someone fill me in?" It takes courage to stop by a coworker's desk and ask if you can shadow them while they work through the process you need to master.

There are always going to be shitty, insecure people who intentionally misread the bravery of self-awareness, willfully misinterpreting it as a sign of weakness and seizing it as an opportunity to go on the attack. They will try to convince you that you're somehow inferior for trying to learn and grow, and they will suggest that if you were truly intelligent and talented you wouldn't need to ask for help.

Ignore them. Don't even try to argue with them or convince them they're wrong—just cheerfully dismiss whatever nonsense they're spewing and go back to being your rising-star self.

### A&Q

While there's nothing wrong with flat-out requesting information if that's what you really need, you'll probably get more mileage out of your interactions with more experienced coworkers if you try coming up with answers on your own before consulting them. You're trying to develop your capacity to make smart choices, and testing your instincts is a way to train yourself more effectively.

"How do I do X?" gives you some useful information, but only about how your coworker would handle things. An approach like "I'm planning on accomplishing X by doing A, B, and then C—what do you think?" will open up a conversation about different perspectives, potentially giving you detailed guidance on how your own thought process might be adjusted. Maybe your colleague would do C before B, but that's more of their personal preference than the official Right Way. Or, maybe you *have* to do B before A, and talking through that will give you a better grasp of the factors to consider in your decision-making.

Finally, on a purely practical note, "give me your take on this situation" is a much more enjoyable interaction than "tell me how to do a thing" for the person on the receiving end, so your relationships with senior colleagues will probably be improved if you save the "help, need info!"–type requests for the times when you're truly clueless.

## If You Don't Know, Now You Know

As more professional responsibility is conferred on you, your position becomes less about your ability to execute particular tasks and more about your ability to think critically about what should be done, who should do it, and when it should happen. Inevitably you're going to make some mistakes as you figure out your own individual approach to a given role. (For more on Mistakes, the Making Of, keep reading.) That is *fine*, just so long as you see those errors as learning experiences and use them to help yourself get better.

This is where the "don't be afraid to ask for help/advice/ mentorship" aspect becomes crucial: while due-diligence research and careful thought can't always prevent a screwup, that prep work will help you explain yourself to the people holding you accountable if things go awry. Whereas if you just charge ahead hoping that you'll magically stumble upon the right course of action, that's a lot harder to justify.

So. Trust yourself, get help when you need it, and never let a fear of being wrong get in the way of an instructive lesson. That's the path toward succeeding in a new role that's a bit of a stretch— and coincidentally, that's pretty much the formula for workplace success in general.

# Surprising Yourself (Remix): Not in a Good Way

*Learning what you're bad at—*
*and learning to live with it*

Dear Businesslady,

So you know how when you're in a job interview, you're asked about whether or not you have any expertise in XYZ, and you're like "no, but I'm sure I'll pick it up quickly"?

I just got a job where the XYZ in question is budgeting/expense management and it turns out that I am T E R R I B L E at that. I also hate it, apparently, but I guess that's not too surprising.

I keep making mistakes and since I'm well past my training/probation period, I can tell my coworkers are starting to worry. I don't know what to do! I can't just be like, "yeah, budgeting, I'm not doing that anymore" but I'm afraid I'm going to seriously screw something up if I keep being in charge of money. (Fortunately all my errors to date have been minorish or caught by someone else before they could get serious, but people are starting to make noise about me becoming more autonomous and I don't know how to discourage them without outing myself as incompetent.)

How can I fix this? I just keep replaying that interview moment in my head and wishing I'd answered "No way, don't let me anywhere near a budget, trust me!" thus avoiding the slow disintegration of my burgeoning career. Do you have any advice and/or a time machine?

—Accounts Inconceivable

→ Oof. This is tough because it's different from growing into a new and challenging role or recovering from a one-off error: you're completely misaligned with your position and need to find a way out.

Even if we'd like to pretend otherwise, talents are not equally distributed across the human population. For example, I have never in my entire life successfully executed a cartwheel—not even back when I was a small child actively enrolled in gymnastics.

When you're new to the workforce, you're often hired based on what you *might* be able to do versus what you've actually *done*. Occasionally, a situation like this arises, which is the professional equivalent of me unwittingly getting hired into a Cirque du Soleil troupe.

When that happens, you need to find a way to escape.

### I'm Not Who You Think I Am

In slightly different circumstances—if you were interested in sticking it out and seeing if you could improve over time—I'd refer you to the previous section. And if you disliked the work despite being reasonably competent at it, I'd council you to grit your teeth for as long as you can stand it while you look for a better position (see "This Isn't Working" in Chapter 7).

But if you're sure that a given position isn't for you *and* you're struggling to do it successfully, then you've got to 'fess up.

True, this will not be a fun conversation for you or for your manager. Realistically, the light at the end of the tunnel might be shining on a newly jobless you. The only alternative, though, is flailing around until you do make a fireable mistake, and that combines the worst-case outcome of raising the issue yourself with all the bad blood that accompanies a termination for cause.

But I'm not saying you should immediately march into your boss's office to declare yourself incompetent.

### Find a Clearly Marked Exit Pathway

One thing you *can* do immediately is start job-searching. It's not great to be on the hunt so soon after getting hired, but if you're looking for other entry-level jobs that don't include your newly discovered Achilles' heel, it shouldn't be too hard to find an interviewer who's sympathetic to "unfortunately it's come to my attention that I'm terrible at [whatever]." If you get lucky, you might find a new position in time to make a seamless departure. And even if you're let go before you've landed a new gig, at least you'll have gotten a head start.

Also—in case my raising the specter of unemployment didn't already make you think of this—start saving whatever money you can, immunizing yourself against a sudden disappearance of income.

### Try (Just a Little Bit Harder)

As your quest for a more agreeable position simmers away, the sense that you're Doing Something should help calm your nerves during the uphill trudge at your current job. Relax, forgive yourself for not being good at every single thing in life, and take every day as its own isolated challenge. Don't worry about what your coworkers think, just triple-check your work and remember that this is a temporary condition that will soon subside.

Yes, I know I said you need to discuss this with your boss ASAP, and you will. But your boss could be out of town, or swamped, or otherwise unavailable for that kind of A Talk™, so you have to find a way to muddle along until the opportunity presents itself.

### It's Not You, It's Me

Once you do have your sit-down with your manager, be succinct, factual, and as upbeat as possible:

- **Explain:** "I am not good at this thing and I'm concerned that my performance will never improve."
- **Point out:** "The organization's best interests are not served by me continuing to do this thing."
- **Emphasize:** "I'm not averse to hard work, and I'm not asking for special treatment by raising this issue."
- **Negotiate:** "If there's a way to move this thing off my plate, I'd be more than happy to take on [whatever tasks need doing that you have reason to believe are within your sphere of expertise]."

- **Empathize:** "I understand that this puts you and [company] in a bad spot and I apologize for misjudging my own abilities during my interview. I truly thought I'd be able to improve with time, but now that I've realized this is a shortcoming of mine I want to address it as soon as possible."

Then, listen. The next steps will be dependent on a constellation of factors: the other open jobs in your organization, the budget for staffing, your manager's personality and how well it meshes with your own, your fit within the office's culture more generally, and the degree to which your manager believes you're capable of shifting to a different set of responsibilities.

### Finding Firmer Ground

In theory, you might be asked to pack up your desk right then and there. Or, in a slightly less grim but nevertheless not-great turn of events, you might be given a little while to wrap up your current projects before you part ways with this particular job.

It won't be a picnic in the event that you find yourself jobless, but hopefully you can negotiate a good reference—or at least a lukewarm one along the lines of "well, she tried her best"—and if you can get them to treat it as a layoff, you can collect unemployment (which isn't an option if you quit voluntarily or are fired for Serious Reasons).

But that's the worst-case scenario. Unless there's really no other place for you, there's a decent chance you'll be able to resettle in a different position that's more in line with your strong suits.

Either way, you'll be free. Free of the pervasive sense of failure, and free to start developing your talents in a new vocation.

# In the Feedback Loop

*Gracefully accepting criticism, responding to it, and moving on*

Dear Businesslady,

I'm in a role that's a stretch for me, so I'm learning a lot, but I'm also making a lot of newbie errors that my manager has been drawing to my attention. All seems well overall, but I have some kind of complex about receiving criticism no matter how gently it's delivered. Even something basic like "that e-mail you copied me on sounded fine, but I think it would've been better broken up into several short paragraphs" has me feeling anxious and guilty for hours.

Basically, every time my boss pulls me aside to give me feedback, I want to burst into tears. I *did* actually burst into tears once, during a performance evaluation that included some tough love, and while my manager was nice about it I could tell she was taken aback. How can I handle this stuff more appropriately? In the past, I didn't care about my job nearly as much so I could just let criticism roll off my back. Now, I guess I care *too* much, and I'm afraid it's making me sabotage myself.

—Feedback: Can't Live With or Without It

➡ The good news is that you're invested in doing your job well (always a positive), but the bad news is that you're being way too hard on yourself. Not so much that it's officially a Problem—yet—but enough that it'll start to work against you if you don't find a middle ground between antipathy and overreaction.

## Feedback Is a Gift

There may be inherently mean people out there who get a secret (or not-so-secret) thrill out of making other people feel crappy—for whom the chance to point out someone else's mistake or missed opportunity for greatness is like finding a surprise $20 at the bottom of a purse.

But we're not really talking about them, except to point out that they suck.

For most of us, it's not fun or easy to say "hey, here's how that could've gone better." Managers *know* their employees aren't eager to be criticized—they know because they get feedback too, and in fact they're often passing along the same advice that they received earlier in their own careers. But they do it anyway.

It might seem appealing to imagine having a boss who never tells you the hard truths, who just sort of shrugs at your missteps while giving you praise when you truly exceed. To be fair, that is indeed preferable to having a jerk boss who's actively mean.

But a manager who takes the time to offer constructive criticism is going out of their way to mentor *without you even having to ask.* They're doing it even though it might piss you off in the moment, or make you feel bad, or frustrate you. They're doing it because they believe you have the power to do better, and helping you achieve that potential is more important to them than being seen as your cool office buddy.

Sure, they're also probably trying to increase profits or page views or whatever your organization's goals are, too (I'm not *that* naïve), but if they're trying to help you improve, that's still something that will benefit you if you bother to listen.

So, if you start feeling affronted by some negative feedback—or guilty or self-flagellate-y or any other unpleasant emotion—try to remember that it really, truly, is for your own good.

## No More Tears

Of course, knowing that feedback is beneficial doesn't automatically change how you react to it. And when you put your inner crybaby in charge of "responding to criticism," that disincentivizes people from giving you advice in the future. We all have bad days, and if you do find tears materializing during a conversation with your manager, it's not the end of the world—as long as you convey "I realize this is inappropriate."

For some low-level eye-watering/lip-trembling, just take a moment to collect yourself. If you start full-on bawling, then excuse yourself from the meeting entirely and follow up when you're more composed.

Either way, once you're calmer, apologize for letting your emotions get away from you and stress that you're grateful for your manager's input. If it becomes a trend, then you need to throw in a hearty dose of "I'm really trying to work on this" along with a demonstrable effort to curtail it going forward.

By pointing this out, I'm not trying to embarrass people with hair-trigger tear ducts. I used to be terrible at hearing anything other than praise without sobbing, and while I've managed to keep it together in my professional life to date (knock wood) I sympathize with how infuriating it is to feel like your own face and body are betraying you.

The fact remains, though, that you can't cry at work. At least, not anywhere outside your own closed-door office or the bathroom (especially if the catalyst is a work-related issue). The law of the land requires you to keep your feels under wraps while in public, and so you must obey.

## Take It Impersonally

Once you've mastered the art of stoically accepting criticism, the next step is to use it to your advantage. It's great to have an employee who's naturally good at a handful of things—but if they're capable of getting *better*, and becoming proficient at *new* things, that's an employee a savvy manager will go to great lengths to keep.

You want to be that kind of employee.

So, whenever any aspect of your performance is critiqued, listen attentively. Take notes you can refer to later, and make sure you're really grasping the issue that your boss (or whoever) is raising.

If you think the conversation might benefit from an analysis of the reasons behind your actions, then feel free to share them—but be careful to avoid the impression that you're making excuses or being defensive. The goal isn't to argue your side, but rather to suss out whether there's a flaw in your rationale that, once corrected, will help prevent similar mistakes in the future.

### Take It to Heart

Once you have received The Feedback, drill it into your brain. Even if it's something minor, you'll feel a lot worse (and be a lot more justified in feeling that way) if your boss has to tell you the same thing twice.

When the opportunity presents itself, point out to your manager that you're implementing the advice they gave you: "I know you thought the last client e-mail was too wall-of-text, so I've tried to break this one up into easily digestible pieces." That shows you're paying attention *and* that you're making the most of the suggestions you're given, which will both encourage further feedback and raise your boss's opinion of you in general.

Take it from me—no one ever becomes so fantastic at their job that they're immune to criticism. The most successful people are the ones who don't let critique sour their workplace relationships. Instead, they harness it, and use it in order to keep getting better.

# The Worst That Could Happen

*Recovering from a significant mistake*

Dear Businesslady,

What's the protocol for moving on after you've screwed up royally at work? Bluntly put, I fucked up. I was organizing a trip for my boss and I somehow completely forgot to book her hotel. In New York City. During a week when apparently everyone else on the planet was also in town.

I realized the oversight a day before the trip, which had otherwise been planned months in advance. I frantically tried to find her a place to stay on short notice, but the only available rooms were either actively disgusting or literally thousands of dollars a night. And so I had to confess.

In the end, we ended up canceling—my boss wasn't about to stay at the YMCA and we couldn't afford to drop $50 grand on lodging. Her meetings got scrapped, so my stupid mistake caused a ripple effect across the calendars of a bunch of high-ranking people who are now understandably frustrated with our organization. We had to pay for the nonrefundable airfare we booked, too.

And it's all. my. fault.

I've heard all the platitudes—people are sometimes happy to get an unexpected hour free, a few hundred bucks on airfare is pretty minor, and it'll all be forgotten someday. Fine. I still feel awful and queasy every time I think about it, and now that's affecting my ability to focus on work (when the last thing I need is to make another dumb screwup!). How do I get on with my life, and how do I make sure I don't ever, EVER, do something like this again?

—Living the Nightmare

➤ Ahh, the big-time mistake. Anyone who's held a job with any level of responsibility will be treated to this experience eventually, and there's really nothing like it: the cold chill down your spine as you realize what you've done, the desperate and futile attempt to correct it without anyone noticing, and the hot flush of shame as you reluctantly confess your integral role in the shit hitting the fan.

It is the worst. It is demoralizing. And it is pretty much inevitable.

## Shit Happens

Obviously you want to do your best to avoid being a chronic mistake-maker—via double-checking, list-making, proofreading, or whatever else has the potential to help you avert disasters.

Nevertheless, it's true: mistakes are made. The only foolproof way to prevent them is to either (a) be perfect or (b) never do anything ever. Both are pretty impractical for the modern workplace.

So don't beat yourself up for experiencing one of the inescapable setbacks of professional life. I know, I know—when you're the one shouldering the blame, whatever you did feels like the flagship failing in the history of office jobs. But it really will fade with time.

## The Worse the Experience, the Better the Story

One of my earliest yay-maybe-I-can-support-myself-through-working-after-all jobs was as a CEO's assistant, and one day I managed to mess up my boss's calendar so that he went to a lunch meeting a week before the other person was scheduled to join him—causing him to waste an hour and a half of a busy day for no reason. (This was in ye olden dayes when businesspeople didn't carry tiny e-mail-checkers in their pockets, and it took a while for us to connect by phone so I could realize, and then explain, what had happened.) Even worse, he walked to and from the restaurant—unnecessarily, mind you!—while recovering from a broken toe.

Having written that out, it doesn't even sound that bad, right? But when it happened, I felt like I had basically ruined my entire career. I *still* feel some echo of that sensation at the memory, even though it's long subsided into the hazy historical mist of "things that don't matter anymore."

## Freakouts Solve No Problems

I'd like to say that was my last professional screwup, but that would be a lie. What has changed since then, though, is that now I waste less time being paralyzed with fear and guilt whenever things go seriously haywire.

Mistakes are inherently beyond your control, but you *can* control your response, which should be to immediately start fixing the problems they've caused. The sooner you can jump in to help with the recovery effort, the better. You can't do that while you're stricken with self-doubt, and if you turn your error into The Saga of How I Must Now Be Reassured of My Worth, you're only going to make things worse. Instead, distract yourself by moving forward and minimizing any aftershocks.

## A Learning Experience

Once you've done the requisite damage control and your initial feelings of horror have dwindled away, then you can investigate strategies for preventing a similar mistake in the future. Sometimes, you'll realize that there was a key fail-safe you failed to implement and you can adjust your process accordingly—something to point out to your manager as you reassure them there won't be a second time.

Sadly, and often, your mistake postmortem will just teach you something you already knew, like "read things closely." And so, you just . . . try to do better. You stay on your best behavior and work extra carefully until the sting of failure wears away.

Either way, you apologize to everyone within the blast radius of the screwup, vow to avoid a repeat performance, and do whatever you can to make amends with whoever was affected.

Most mistakes, in most jobs, aren't going to be so catastrophic that they preclude any hope of a second chance. So as long as you accept responsibility, maintain an otherwise high level of performance, and learn whatever lessons are there to be learned, all will eventually be forgiven and (hopefully) forgotten.

# Wipe That Face Off Your Face

*Maintaining a good attitude even when
you're justifiably annoyed*

Dear Businesslady,

I guess I have an attitude problem, but I'm not sure I even care about fixing it. My boss and I do not get along, at all, and I'm just trying to get through the days before I leave for something better (although I'm still looking so who knows how long it'll be before I can escape).

He's a micromanager and his style could be charitably described as "abrasive." All of his critiques are delivered with zero nuance or delicacy, and he obsesses over the tiniest things (like, "I've told you not to use the word 'impactful'"–level nitpicky). His unending tirades about everything I do wrong now include attacks on my actual personality, because I'm not all sweetness and light while he's tearing down everything I do.

People talk about "maintaining a positive attitude"—but the last time I checked, you can't control your feelings. I'm not sure I even have a question here, but if I did, I guess it would be, is there any hope for people like me who just aren't naturally bubbly? I'm realistic enough to know I'll have other crappy bosses in my life, and the idea of being harangued about my demeanor throughout the rest of my career is really depressing.

—Could You Just NOT?!

➤ You can't control your feelings but you can control how you express them. And openly displayed annoyance is definitely an office taboo.

This isn't about silently tolerating abuse or biting your tongue instead of standing up for yourself. (There are ways to call out bullshit while remaining professional, which I'll discuss at length in Chapters 5 and 6.) This is about following the social conventions of the workplace and—crucially—preventing yourself from standing in the way of your own success.

## Feedback Is a Gift—But Some Gifts Are Crappy

While feedback is intended to improve your performance, that doesn't mean you'll always agree with or even understand it. The greatest of managers are still occasionally going to tear apart a project you were proud of, make you change something you thought was perfect as-is, or issue instructions you think are a fundamentally bad idea. You can voice your disagreement, but when you reach the impasse of "I'm the boss and you're not," then you inwardly sigh and let them win. (And if it turns out you were right all along, you draw upon your inner strength and refrain from saying "I told you so.")

## You Wouldn't Like Me When I'm Cranky

Again—you *inwardly* sigh. You do not outwardly sigh, nor do you roll your eyes, say something snotty, or complain to a coworker (except with extreme caution).

You don't have to like your manager—technically, you don't even have to respect them. What you need to respect is your manager's pivotal role in your continued employment.

Conveying anything on the spectrum of "contempt" toward your boss will only work against you. They may be stoic enough not to care about it personally, but they absolutely *will* care that you're disrespecting their authority, making the office less pleasant, and making their job more difficult. It's a surefire way to end up on your manager's shit list and ensure you're last in line for promotions, raises, or any other potential perks. And that's the best-case scenario—if you're being egregiously insubordinate, you could also just get straight-up fired for it.

There's a reason that "if you don't have anything nice to say, don't say anything at all" is drilled into us since childhood. It's not fun to be around someone who's an endless fountain of negativity. And anyone with the power to distance themselves from such a person—i.e., a manager—is going to exercise it. Even if they're not consciously trying to retaliate, you'll become the natural choice if they need to shunt someone off into an isolated department or eliminate a position. Moreover, they're certainly not going to bother mentoring and nurturing someone who radiates hostility.

Some people aren't destined to get along with each other, and that's fine. If your boss irritates you to the point that you're quivering with rage every time you interact, then it's probably wise to start looking around for a new job that's a better fit. In the meantime, clench your teeth and keep it cordial.

### Reinventing Venting

There are benefits to having work friends—they can improve your morale immeasurably whenever you need a sympathetic ear. But you need to be judicious about confiding in them whenever you're exasperated with management.

Now, look: I'm not an unreasonable person. I know that "complaining about your boss" is often the way office friendships get formed, and I'm not going to take that off the table as a bonding activity.

It just can't be the only thing you talk about, or it will quickly get toxic. Save it for the major issues.

Fixating on your manager's annoying habits and questionable decisions will soon cloud your judgment to the point that their every action seems worthy of mockery. And you won't be the only one infected by this negativity—your whole circle of snark will start feeling the same way. It may be fun in the moment to issue an epic takedown of your boss's latest weird behavior, but in the big picture it helps create a sense that you work in a crappy place run by crappy people. Even if that is in fact the case, there's no benefit to lingering on your job's worst aspects.

Vent your frustrations to your coworkers only when you really need to: when you're truly curious about their take on a situation, when you're so pissed off that you desperately need an outlet, or when something's so absurd that you know they'll find it hilarious (see, I'm not a monster). But cut yourself off from going down a rabbit hole of "every little thing boss does is bullshit" and try to encourage your friends to do the same. Giving in to that perspective will only make it harder for you to maintain a civil attitude—and if your coworkers can't be trusted to keep your less-than-politic observations to themselves, the consequences could be even more dire.

## An Arsenal of Appropriateness

So, how do you keep your cool when you desperately want to throw a stapler at your boss's face? The specific contours of your polite-ified interactions will be determined by your broader personality, but here are some ideas to help you get started.

If you feel an eye-roll or scowl coming on, try to raise your eyebrows and pull the corners of your mouth up into something resembling a smile. It might feel fake—it might even look fake—but that's still an improvement on an active glower. (Note that this isn't about counteracting "resting bitch face" or adhering to some icky standard of constant, mandatory smiling—it's about preventing your specific face from telegraphing negative emotions against your will.)

Avoid monosyllabic responses like "sure" or "fine"—it's too easy for irritation to attach itself to those without you even hearing it. More enthusiastic replies like "absolutely," "right away," and "of course"—delivered in the most pleasant tone you can muster—will help obscure whatever derisive commentary is running through your head. Mentally append an exclamation point to things. Anyone with a background in retail or waiting tables should be adept at this flavor of forced cheeriness, and there's no reason those same skills can't be transferred to an office context.

It might also be useful to consider that your boss may be dealing with their own stresses—including unreasonable demands from a workplace overlord who outranks them. Even if that's not actually true, remembering that they're probably not being obnoxious *on purpose* could defuse some of your frustration.

Finally, be kind to yourself and prepare accordingly when you know you're about to endure a taxing situation. Before meeting with a manager you loathe, make sure you're well fed, sufficiently caffeinated, and as relaxed as you can possibly be. It's a lot harder to avoid seeming annoyed when you walk in with a metaphorical rain cloud over your head.

### Best Actor

Once you've made a habit of masking your truest, crankiest feelings, it might actually start to feel natural—possibly preventing some of that vitriol from bubbling up in the first place.

Even if you never get used to maintaining a neutral game face at work, still keep trying. You're not doing it to spare your boss's feelings—you're doing it for you, to ensure you stay on the good side of the powers that be. You're also doing it for your less-objectionable coworkers, as a way of mitigating the inherent challenges of holding down a job.

## CHAPTER 4

## YOUR TIME WON'T MANAGE ITSELF:
# Staying on Task—and Staying Sane

FOR MOST OF us, our earliest jobs basically entail being a warm body: stay here and watch my kid while I go out, stand here and make peoples' sandwiches to order, wait here at the cash register until someone's ready to check out. You show up, you perform the requisite tasks, and then you leave when your time is up. The next day, same thing.

By contrast, as you start taking on more responsibilities, you're given a corresponding amount of authority over how you spend your day. Are you at your best first thing in the morning, but useless after lunch? Or do you need a good half-hour of lighthearted chitchat and several cups of coffee before you make any attempts at productivity? Can this project wait a couple of days, or is it really urgent? If that thing isn't due for a few weeks, when should you get started on it? And—in today's increasingly connected and technologized world—when's the cutoff for saving an e-mail for tomorrow?

Now, you're not the sole arbiter of these decisions. The actual answers will depend on all kinds of factors, most notably your workplace's culture and the expectations that go along with it. Still, there's usually some leeway in how you approach your job *as you*, and if you don't reassess your system every now and again, you're setting yourself up for a lot of personal stress, and maybe even a little professional disaster.

There are always going to be instances when a deadline collides with a crisis and everything is awful for a while. But work shouldn't feel nightmarishly difficult by default, and it shouldn't leave you struggling to find room in your schedule for fun and relaxation. If that's your daily reality, you could probably benefit from a few process adjustments aimed at making your professional life a little less harrowing.

I don't have One Weird Lifehack that will permanently abolish anxiety, but I can help you find time-management strategies that fit your particular style.

# Step One: Make a List

## *Juggling multiple priorities without getting overwhelmed*

Dear Businesslady,

I recently moved up from an admin role—where my daily workload was basically stimulus:response w/r/t whatever my various superiors needed—to one where I'm (frighteningly) at liberty to control my own schedule. I'm happy to have landed in this position but I find myself staying awake nights, stressing about all the different things on my plate. I deal with a lot of deadlines, some far out in the future and some that pop up urgently due to circumstances beyond my control. I'm so accustomed to just doing whatever is asked of me on any given day, it's hard for me to avoid feeling like I'm failing if anything stays unfinished—and then at the same time, I get freaked out over projects I know are on the horizon, but which I don't have time to deal with yet.

I am actually, literally losing sleep over this stuff, and I don't want to talk to anyone at work about it in case they decide I'm not actually ready for the level of autonomy they've given me. How do I manage this??

—Stress Dreams Are Made of These

➤ This is such a common problem, especially if you're transitioning from a more reactive role to a more proactive one. In certain jobs, your entire purpose is to handle things immediately, but that's not a practical approach for every position—and if you hold yourself to that standard when it's not actually required, you're going to do worse work (while also making yourself miserable). So how do you find a balance between constant diligence and letting go? For starters, you need a system for organizing your portfolio of tasks.

### Brains Are for Thinking; Lists Are for Remembering

Inside your skull there is a supercomputer of tremendous power, but its user interface is wonky at best. Sometimes it shuts down at crucial moments due to poor nutritional input or insufficient rest periods, and sometimes it will seize on an insipid commercial jingle and play it on repeat for hours. It has a search function, but it usually only turns up results hours later, typically right when you're about to fall asleep. And it can produce negative emotional states that screw up your whole day for no reason.

Still, it has its perks—it's waterproof, for one, and the battery life is pretty decent, all things considered.

Since you can't control your mind's processing procedure, you have to find ways to work around its quirks. Your brain tries its hardest to keep tabs on everything you need to do—sometimes even successfully. But brains are terrible at prioritizing, so "figure out where that 2 P.M. meeting's being held" and "prepare the report that's due in six months" can end up consuming an equal amount of attention and energy. To avoid forgetting anything, your mind is just spinning indefinitely on the same things over and over, making your workload feel far more vast than it actually is.

Whenever I'm feeling exceptionally anxious and overwhelmed by work, it's invariably because I need a to-do list. Once you actually see all the tasks laid out in front of you, it's easy to triage them based on urgency, importance, and your overall workflow. When they're all just rattling around in your head, every single thing gets counted multiple times, and there's no way to distinguish the minor stuff from what's actually worth worrying about.

You might *think* you don't want to make a list, because then you'll be confronted with all the things you have to do and feel even more stressed out. But—well, first of all, denial is rarely a smart strategy in any situation, but besides that—some part of you is already aware of all that stuff, and you're expending extra brainpower trying to keep it all organized without a reference document. Even if you look at your to-do list and think "holy shit, this is a lot," I guarantee it will feel more manageable than it did before you wrote it all down.

### And You *Do* Need to Write It Down

For any readers who reject the idea of to-do lists (or calendars, their close cousins), I get it—I used to be one of you. As someone with a decent memory, for a long time I thought writing stuff down was just an extra, unnecessary step. That's because I was dealing with a pretty small sample size of information, enough that it didn't overtax my recall capacity. Plus, I hadn't yet figured out the relationship between mental anguish and untracked tasks, so I just assumed I was stressed because I had a stressful job (which, admittedly, was also true).

I can't say exactly when I started losing my grasp on my calendar and my to-be-done work—when it started feeling like too much to handle without external support—but I know it happened. Afterward it was a slow, uphill battle to develop a system for recording appointments and keeping tabs on whatever tasks were outstanding. It feels natural now, but it took a while to figure out an approach that would actually work, so you'll be better off developing those habits from day one.

### Optimize Your Operating System

Now, for me, "a to-do list" almost always means an actual, physical list: usually a piece of 8½" × 11" scrap paper folded in half on which I've written things down with pen. And this isn't (just) because I'm a withered crone.

I've tried time and again to switch to a more electronic, twenty-first-century method, and inevitably what happens is this: I forget to look at it. And then my brain, grateful that I've relieved it of the burden of remembering what needs to get done, forgets about that stuff entirely—until I wake up in the middle of the night with the sudden realization there's a doc somewhere listing a bunch of stuff I've been emphatically not doing.

If you're a tech aficionado who never met a productivity app you didn't love, then more power to you—I'm not trying to suggest that analog is the only way to go. Feel free to play around with different programs to see which ones match your style. Or go on the ol' Google, see what's being touted as the be-all end-all solution to organization this week, and test it out. You just need to find a system—any system—that integrates seamlessly with your own personal work routine.

### Have List, Still Stressed

"This is bullshit," I hear some of you yelling. "My entire monitor is covered in Post-it reminders and I'm still always freaked out about work!" Okay, sure, the act of list-making alone isn't going to make everything fall into place for you. But it gives you the information you'll need in order to plan your time most efficiently.

Or, maybe the source of your anxiety isn't a lack of organization, but it's *something* fixable, and we'll cover those other stressors in later chapters.

### What Do We Have Here Now?

After you've organized all your tasks and deadlines, you can start thinking strategically about when to tackle individual line items. Really urgent stuff is in some ways the easiest: Do it ASAP. But for slower-burning projects, you'll want to consider a few factors: When are you going to *want* to do them? When do they really need to be finished, and can you give yourself a buffer in case something else comes up right at the deadline?

Sometimes it's perfectly reasonable to say, "I'm not even going to think about X until Y and Z are done." But if you're putting something off, you need to make sure you've thought through all the steps involved. If completing X means gathering info from fifteen different people and booking a bunch of conference rooms, then it's worth taking a few minutes to send off the necessary e-mails and get the ball rolling—even if you have no intention of doing the real *work* yet.

By thinking about the big picture, you'll make sure your carefully calibrated workflow doesn't hit any last-minute snags. Periodically review your to-do list to see if there's any "set it and forget it" processing you can start up for the stuff that you're ignoring in favor of more time-sensitive projects. Your future self will thank you.

# Just Send the Damn E-Mail Already

*Some anti-procrastination techniques*

Dear Businesslady,

I am a procrastinator.

It sucks.

I expend way more energy worrying about things I haven't done yet—that I've let go for far too long—than I actually expend in finally getting around to them.

Clearly I'm self-aware enough to realize this, but then I spend yet another workday glued to my Snapchat feed. I feel this constant, gross background anxiety about the various un-done tasks that anyone could ask me about at any time (forcing me to come up with an excuse that wouldn't get me fired), but when the moment comes to actually deliver, it all seems so unimportant and like I have infinite time.

I somehow manage to get stuff done once I truly can't put it off any longer, but doing everything last-minute is super stressful. What can I do to get work done on a regular basis, instead of this weird whiplash between manic bursts of productivity and profound stasis?

—Letting the Days of My Life Pass By

The only antidote for the type of procrastinatory inertia you describe is to actually make some real progress on your work—but I realize that "get up and do something" is easier said than done.

This problem could have a few potential causes—magical thinking, an insufficiently challenging job, bad work habits—and in some cases, it may not even be a problem at all (really!). Whatever the origin, I have a bunch of self-motivation techniques to help you overcome it.

### A Worker at Work Stays at Work; A Worker at Rest Stays at Rest

That's Businesslady's First Law of Productivity. For basic-level "but I don't *wanna*"–type procrastination, getting motivated is a lot like jump-starting a car: once you're doing something, anything, that's vaguely worklike, it's easier to keep on going.

When you're having a particularly demotivated moment, pick the simplest, most no-brainer thing on your to-do list (or the most enjoyable, if you're lucky enough to have anything in that category) and take care of it. It's fine if it's not particularly pressing—this is about rebooting your perspective, not finding the perfect sequence of task-completion. It's about reminding you how satisfying it feels to get shit done.

### Wave of Motivation

Once you've got a rhythm going, move on to the next thing. And then the next. Eventually you need to start paying attention to deadlines and urgency, but as long as you're not totally disregarding those things, you're fine. You're crossing things off your list, you're winnowing down your inbox, you're setting things in motion for future projects, whatever.

This is especially useful if there's some Big Complicated Thing that you keep putting off because it seems like a huge pain in the ass (or because you're awaiting the mythical "right moment" to dive in). Force yourself to get started on it—with the option to immediately abandon it if you want to—and see what happens. Whenever I finally tackle a project I've been dreading, it's pretty much always easier than I expected it to be. And on the rare occasions it isn't—when I'm like "oh yeah, I remember why I've been avoiding this for so long"—I'm still grateful for the opportunity to do it piecemeal rather than in one agonizing burst of activity right at the deadline. Once you've started chipping away at a massive undertaking, it becomes less massive, and therefore less intimidating.

### Tomorrow and Tomorrow and Tomorrow

Don't get me wrong: I've accomplished many a task through a frenetic pre-deadline whirlwind. But that can't be your only strategy for getting things done. The unpredictability of life is pretty well documented at this point, so you can't rule out the possibility that you might suffer some strange personal catastrophe on the day you'd finally set aside for Project X.

More importantly—and more realistically—you can't do everything at the last minute because you never know what other work-related tasks might arise. A coworker might quit or go on medical leave, leaving you suddenly assigned to pick up the slack, or your boss might resurrect a previously completed project and have you entirely redo it. Even in the most structured jobs, there are always breaks in the routine, and if you blow a deadline every time the unexpected happens, your manager will start to question whether you can handle autonomy. Plus, your colleagues will get frustrated if you're always behind on things, turning stuff in late, or obviously fluctuating between periods of slackerdom and frantic catch-up.

Even if you can magically convert yourself into a hyperproductive person in certain scenarios, reserve that superpower for special occasions, and try to goad yourself into working more consistently overall.

### What If We Didn't Call It "Procrastination"?

There will always be times when you're just not feeling the whole "getting work done" thing. Guess what? That's perfectly fine.

Seriously! It's not always a bad thing to procrastinate (even if that term itself has an unavoidably negative connotation). If you're responsible for a task that will take you two hours, and there are five business days between you and the deadline, it's not irresponsible for you to stall on completing it—especially if you've got other, higher-priority stuff to work on in the meantime. Again, you're in charge of your own workflow, and that means you're within your rights to decide when particular stuff gets worked on.

You've gotta be realistic about what you're asking of yourself. Everyone's energy ebbs and flows throughout the day, and while the sudden appearance of a super-crucial task might give you the adrenaline boost you need to tackle it, you can't fool yourself into believing something's time sensitive when it's not. Letting projects creep perilously close to their deadlines is a way of generating a real sense of urgency—and the motivation that comes along with it.

However, if you're going to indulge in some downtime, make sure you're actually enjoying it. Leaving the office at 2 P.M. to go do something fun can be a great way to recharge and hit the ground running the next day. By contrast, if you spend all afternoon half-assedly reading BuzzFeed and feeling simultaneously guilty and bored, it's not like you get brownie points for remaining at your desk. You're not getting any more work done in the second scenario, but you're going to feel a lot crappier about your job and life in general when the clock finally says 5:00. (Believe me, I know this from experience.) So if you're taking a break, make sure it's really a *break*, not just the absence of productivity.

### A Slow Year

If you're *always* bored, and relying on procrastination to inject some excitement into your job, then something's gotta change. Unless you enjoy the easy-breezy vibe of your position, ask your boss for more responsibility. Chances are, there are plenty of overworked coworkers who'd be happy to transfer some tasks to your purview. And if you strike out there, well, at least your underwhelming workload will make it easy to conduct a job search and find your way into a gig that's more stimulating.

# Your Phone Has a Silent Mode

*Finding the right work/life balance*

Dear Businesslady,

I'm writing on behalf of my friends and family, all of whom regularly give me shit about being "on call" for my job whenever we're trying to spend time together. I work in PR, which means I'm pretty much constantly responding to unexpected crises and client needs on short notice and expected to be available outside normal business hours (early mornings, late nights, weekends, vacations, etc.). I'm still fairly junior, so I'm eager to prove myself and not develop a reputation as someone who's unreachable when I'm needed.

The downside, of course, is that I'm developing a reputation in my private life as someone who's "always on her phone" and on some level I know I could probably dial back without the world falling apart. My supervisor, who is basically who I want to be when I grow up, is great about disconnecting when she needs to, so I know it can be done. But when my phone's dead or I leave it at home, I don't feel free—I feel even *more* anxious, which defeats the purpose of unplugging in the first place. And I live in fear of the day when I decide to go offline only to find out that something major went down in my absence.

How can I shut down that part of my brain (but then still turn it back on again when I need it)?

—Addicted to Workahol

➤ Oh man, I've got some great advice for you! You just need to … {picture me looking down at my phone} … um, just a second … {thumbs frantically tapping} … sorry, almost done … {more tapping} … one more sec … okay! Now what was your question again, something about your commute?

I think I've made my point.

The ubiquity of handheld devices has basically turned us all into assholes. Everyone knows how annoying it is to talk with someone whose attention is at least 50 percent phone-directed, and yet we all end up doing some version of this from time to time. When you're inevitably called out for rudeness, "sorry, *it's work*" feels so self-righteous that it's hard to resist. (Plus, it's a more compelling justification than "sorry, got a new follower on Instagram"— but ultimately they're both essentially the same behavior.)

## Resisting Temptation

We use "workaholic" as a cultural shorthand for "someone who works a lot," but there's a reason it's a spinoff of "alcoholic." Even before phones became computers that reward us with stimuli every time we check them, people have been addicted to working— and I don't invoke the concept of addiction cavalierly. It's appealing, it can be downright *intoxicating*, to feel so important and needed by your job that you can't possibly divert your energy elsewhere.

As with all addictions, your desire to remain connected to work can become a compulsion despite your best intentions—some unconscious part of you might thrive on that sense of importance. Enter the smartphone, which is practically designed to pull you back into a work mindset against your will.

If I had a dollar for every time I went to do something "fun" on my phone (check movie showtimes, look up a factoid that's under discussion, find a photo to show someone, whatever), only to accidentally end up looking at my work e-mail, I'd … have so many dollars that I could go buy a private island somewhere with abysmal cellphone reception. But I don't get a dollar. Instead, I just get distracted from the thing I was doing and reimmersed in the world of professional obligations. Seeing a work e-mail alters your night, even if there's no urgency whatsoever. As you try to wrench yourself back into relaxation mode, a voice in your brain is whispering "you're gonna have to e-mail those drafts to Dana tomorrow" and it'll be a while before you stop hearing it.

One remedy for this problem would be to hurl your smartphone into a fountain or join me on my hypothetical private island. Or, for a more practical solution, you can tweak the way you use your phone when you're off the clock.

Tweak how, you ask? Here are some ideas.

Actually close your e-mail program so it's not the first thing you see when you grab your phone, or at least hide your work inbox. Mute office-related text threads, turn off Slack notifications, and otherwise do what you can to avoid the unwanted intrusion of worky thoughts into your precious private time.

In some jobs, some industries, and in some particularly busy periods, there might be an expectation that you'll be reachable at a moment's notice—but in the vast majority of cases, ignoring evening and overnight e-mails will, at worst, just give you some stuff to do first thing the next day.

### Make 'Em Wait

I can already hear some of you balking at this advice. "You don't understand," you're saying, "in my job, I really do need to respond to every e-mail *right away*." Well, maybe. But allow me to propose the counterpoint of "Are you sure about that?"

Even during the traditional 8-to-5 workday, your job isn't just to monitor your inbox and shoot off replies. You have meetings to go to, non-e-mail stuff to write, plans to brainstorm—you know, actual *work*.

An unanswered e-mail feels like an obligation (and often, it actually is one). It's natural to want to take care of it as quickly as possible so that you don't have to worry about it anymore. Sometimes that's the right call, too—if you want to quickly type up a "sounds great" as an easy way of keeping your inbox clear, I'm not going to stop you.

Not every response is as simple as "sounds great," though, and often your "let me send this real quick" turns into a much longer endeavor. That's true whether you're sitting at your desk or hunched over your phone in a grocery store aisle—but only one of those is going to result in an irritated shopping companion and/or rapidly melting ice cream. Once you start training yourself to let things sit during the workday, it'll start to feel more natural during your downtime.

If you still don't believe me, let's do a quick thought experiment. Think about the last time you sent someone a work-related e-mail—a non-urgent one. Think about how long it took for you to receive a reply. Finally, think about the time after you hit Send, and how much of it you spent eagerly anticipating a response.

. . . none, right? None time? For most of us, unless there are additional stakes attached to an e-mail, it's forgotten the instant we send it out into the world. (And even if there is some reason you're anxiously awaiting a reply, that doesn't necessarily obligate the recipient to get back to you quickly—"please, reassure me that I did a good job on this" doesn't generate actual urgency.)

Get in the habit of figuring out the reasonable turnaround time for every e-mail you receive, and allow yourself to reply at your actual convenience. Once you've tested my hypothesis and confirmed that your office won't disintegrate due to your lack of immediate responsiveness, you'll have the confidence to remain fully present in your personal life.

### Not There, Don't Care

I'm focusing on e-mail because it's a consistent generator of workplace obligations and also something most of us have (constant, arguably excessive) access to. But obviously professional preoccupations can take many forms. And no matter how much you *want* to disconnect, you're never going to actually be able to do it if you don't (a) identify what triggers you into distraction and (b) take steps to avoid those triggers.

You also have to make your peace with the theoretical possibility that you'll miss the occasional urgent e-mail that hits your Inbox at 9 P.M. on a Thursday. Because, yeah, sometimes stuff comes up, and sometimes you have a pang of regret that you weren't available to stamp out a crisis in the moment it emerged. But first of all, let's be honest—you're unlikely to take this advice wholeheartedly, and chances are good that you're gonna see, and respond to, that 9 P.M. e-mail anyway. Even if you don't, what's the real consequence there? Most organizations are able to deal with the fact that people go to concerts, spend time with their families, eat uninterrupted meals, fall asleep. If it's a true emergency and you're really needed, there's always that "call" function that most cellphones still have nowadays—and if you're actually unreachable, one of your colleagues can handle things this time around.

No one's ever going to *complain* if you're responsive around the clock. So if you want to carve out time for yourself, you're going to have to be the one enforcing those boundaries. Trust me when I tell you that it's worth doing.

# Do You Even Know What Kind of Day I've Had??

*Preventing your work life from interfering (too much) with your relationships*

Dear Businesslady,

My job is really stressful. I knew that when I started in this field, but I made it through thanks to my partner—she listened to my tirades about coworker incompetence and patiently took care of all the food prep and housework that I never had time for.

She was able to do these things because she was a grad student. And don't get me wrong, I listened to her when she vented about her PhD program or rude professors. But she was on a more self-directed schedule, and I guess I didn't process how much I came to expect her to put my needs ahead of hers.

Then she got a job of her own. And after the initial rush of "yay, you're a professor now!" wore off, I realized that we'd entered a whole new dynamic. She says she'll be home at 6:30, but a student always shows up right as she's about to leave and by the time she finishes life-coaching them it's 6:45. Then once we're finally together, all she does is rant about work: "Let me spend twenty minutes explaining how they want to restructure the PoliSci curriculum and then spend another twenty minutes explaining my pedagogical objections."

Basically, she's become the "me" in our relationship, and I'm not sure our relationship is sustainable if there are two of us. But then I feel awful—I mean, in addition to being my best friend and someone I've been in love with for nearly a decade, she's the one who's been putting up with my bullshit for years! I feel like a hypocrite, and I don't know what to do.

—Everyone Needs a Housewife, I Guess

➤ Jobs: Is there any kind of domestic problem they *can't* create? Even if you're able to stop yourself from constantly checking work e-mail when you're home, there are a bunch of other insidious ways for a job to disrupt your personal happiness. If you live with someone else (whether it's a romantic partnership, a family household, or a friendly roommate situation), then that bleed-through affects them too.

I can't promise a comprehensive cure for this phenomenon, but I do have some treatment options to help you minimize the symptoms.

### Bringing It All Back Home

It might be tempting to try to keep your professional life and your personal life entirely separate. At some point you need to draw boundaries between them (which I'll get into shortly), so why not make those boundaries massive, impenetrable walls?

I suppose that might work for some people, but I'm pretty convinced that a good partnership involves sharing your experiences of the world with one another. Even if you'd love to put a moratorium on job talk (or you work for, like, the CIA and actually *can't* discuss it), there are always going to be aspects of your career that affect your partner too: your income, when you're home and when you're gone, how much traveling you do, or whether you should relocate to a new city. Your job may be yours alone, but if you keep it entirely to yourself, your household discussions are going to be missing some key information.

### Not Everything Is a Story

Now that I've emphasized the importance of communication, I'm going to emphasize the importance of shutting up sometimes. The deeper you get into a job, the more you become surrounded by minutiae—and that level of detail isn't actually necessary to give someone the gist of what you're dealing with. It will, however, bore your conversational partner to tears, and potentially prompt an unnecessary argument.

It may seem obvious, but learning to bracket the inside-baseball parts of your stories is actually a skill—for both the speaker and the listener. You both just have to accept things like "there's this long stupid process that requires a series of forms" as a setup for the scenario being narrated and leave it at that. Otherwise, you'll spend the entire night describing the process itself, becoming increasingly irritated by follow-up questions. "But isn't that really inefficient?" "Yes! *That's why I said it was stupid, remember??*" "Okay, okay, geez!"

Every once in a while, the backstory will be truly essential, and you'll have to be like, "buckle up as I commence the Saga of the Website Committee." But choose those moments wisely, because your friends and partners—much as they love you, and even though you're truly a delight to converse with—don't have infinite time and patience. You've got to figure out what you really want to talk about and avoid distracting digressions: "My new coworker is annoying," "I was late to a meeting and got yelled at," "They changed the computer system and now it's ridiculously complicated," and all the other exciting adventures of your day.

In all likelihood, the rest of your household wants to regale you with stories too, so staying focused will ensure that you're not constantly performing in the world's most tedious one-person show, all about the intricacies of your workplace.

### Is This Helping?

As you're figuring the core essence of your anecdotes, it's equally worthwhile to figure out why you're compelled to share them—and make sure you and your partner are on the same page. Is it humor? Entertainment? Venting? Complaining? Asking for advice? If you just want to hear "ugh, that's annoying" and instead get a litany of troubleshooting ideas, everyone in the room is going to be exasperated.

It's okay—good even—to be up-front about what you're looking for from a post-work conversation. This is especially true if you happen to be in a relationship with a chronic advice giver (*or so I've heard*) who will compulsively try to "solve" whatever vaguely negative experience you're narrating unless explicitly instructed otherwise (. . . and even then, they might find it challenging to keep silent. Allegedly. Or so my sources have explained). Plus, if you're doing your partner the favor of editing out boring or unnecessary details, their attempts to help might not even be practical, leading to even more easily avoidable irritation.

If you put a little extra thought into the overall arc of your conversations, you'll avoid wasted time, misunderstandings, and the negative emotional energy that's generated when you spend twenty minutes on a long-winded explanation of something that's as aggravating as it is convoluted.

### Closing the Vent

A huge percentage of workplace "storytelling" is really just griping, and that's fine—everyone has crappy days at work, and it can be therapeutic to hear a sympathetic audience commiserate with your professional trials. But you need an exit strategy, because complaining has a powerful momentum. If you begin The Story of How Greg Hums Too Loud, and then a half-hour later you're still saying things like "it's just impossible to think with all that humming going on," it's a sign that you need to switch topics. Sometimes your mood can't change until the subject does.

If you're the vent-ee in this situation, it's a kindness to break the cycle. "Hey, you seem to be getting even more irritated the more we talk about this—wanna go fire up the PlayStation or watch some TV?"

Bad workdays are often hard to shake, so this might not always work. But you can at least try. If you make the mistake of believing that you'll suddenly be flooded with happiness if you complain for just a *little while longer*, you'll end up wasting your whole night on some dumb bullshit.

### Mess Stress

This isn't a housework-advice book, and thank god because that is definitely not my area of expertise. Throughout my time as a job-having person, I've experienced the struggle to uphold some kind of cleanliness standard while also enjoying my downtime as much as possible. Unless you're one of the rare people for whom chores are a stress reliever, a home comprised of working people is a home where certain tradeoffs are constantly being made.

You can buy a different book for tips on keeping your space pleasantly livable, but here are some suggestions for managing the mental/emotional side of housekeeping.

First of all, everyone's busy. Everyone's busy, everyone's tired, and everyone's better at remembering their own contributions to household livability than they are at noticing anyone else's. It's one thing to mention "hey, I did that thing, just so you know" or ask someone else to tackle a task you don't have the energy for. But if you're obsessively tracking all your valiant efforts at cleanliness and simultaneously tallying up all your partner's deficiencies, both of you will be straight-up miserable (and the laundry won't get done any more quickly).

You need to find a system for household maintenance that works with your respective schedules, talents, and preferences, in terms of who typically handles what and what constitutes "clean"—and then you need to be flexible during the periods when the plan goes awry. You need to put in some extra work sometimes, say "leave it for tomorrow" sometimes, and do both from a legit place of generosity. Maintaining a mental scorecard of who's actually pulling their weight (whether or not it's you—but let's be honest, we're all usually the heroes of our own stories) is a waste of mental energy. If your partner or housemate is truly inconsiderate, that will become apparent without any hypervigilance on your part—and then you can buy yet another advice book on avoiding relationships with jerks.

# Home Work

*Successfully working from home:*
*avoiding distractions and staying productive*

Dear Businesslady,

After lobbying my job for months, I finally got authorization to work from home a couple days a week. Hooray! No more 2.5-hour round-trip commute and smelling my cubemate's weird gross lunches. I love my home, I've put a lot of time into making it my perfect space, and I thought using it as an office would be a dream come true.

It . . . isn't.

I love the "being home more" part, of course. But the things that are great about my home are not so great to have in a place while I'm trying to work. There are kitties doing cute things! Chores to randomly get sucked into! And snacks—SOOOO many snacks.

I didn't think of myself as someone who got distracted easily, but apparently I am. I'll lose half my workday to something I never would've even thought to do if I'd actually been "at work," and then I'm scrambling to catch up. Despite my epic commute, I eat dinner later on work-from-home days than office days, because I'm usually behind on work by evening.

For years, I've prided myself on being a proactive, organized, diligent person—but apparently my work-from-home self is just a mess. The other day I nearly missed a Skype meeting because I went out to get the mail and then somehow spent thirty minutes pulling weeds.

I never thought I'd say this, but I'm almost hoping my work-from-home privileges get revoked (and the way things are going, that just might happen).

—Yearning for Cubicle-land

➡ When I've told people "I work from home," I've gotten a variety of reactions—but two of the most common ones are also the most baffling. The first is, "You are *sooooo* lucky," said in a tone of unreserved envy (as opposed to the far less perplexing variations on "that must be nice"). And the second is, "Oh my gosh, how do you do it—I'd never get anything done."

Working from home is definitely a perk, arguably even a privilege—but it has its drawbacks, and it's definitely not an opportunity to draw a salary while luxuriating in the comforts of your living space.

## The Optics of the Situation

Let me start by pointing out that it's entirely possible to sit in a traditional office for eight straight hours and get absolutely nothing done. The idea that being onsite somehow imbues you with magical productivity powers is completely false (unless you're someone who needs that kind of environment in order to generate a sense of motivation—but that's a different thing altogether).

Nevertheless, when you're a remote employee, the fact that you're working is literally invisible to everyone else. Your colleagues can't pop over to your desk to ask a question, they never see you hard at work when they arrive in the morning, and they never see you frantically typing as they're heading out the door. Even if your job is entirely virtual—where you're all just text on screens, voices on phones, and slightly pixelated faces on Skype—that same invisibility still applies.

It's not necessarily a problem, but it's something to keep in mind.

In general, the more unusual your work-from-home situation is, the more you should try to counteract any sense of distance from your coworkers. If you're one of only a few remote employees, it's possible—human nature being what it is—that some of your colleagues are jealous of your schedule flexibility. You aren't responsible for ensuring that everyone at your organization is treated with total equanimity, but if people are looking for reasons to claim that you're just lounging around all day watching Netflix, you don't want to give them that ammunition.

Even if they aren't quietly seething with envy, your coworkers could still have a skewed perspective on your workday. If you haven't gotten back to them on something time sensitive, they may wonder whether you secretly ducked out early to hit the mall. Or you might wind up being the casualty of an innocent mistake—if it's been a while since you weighed in on a collaborative project, maybe they'll forget to invite you to the next planning meeting, but no one will even notice because the in-room headcount is the same as usual.

While you don't need to send e-mails that are just "hey, FYI, still a fellow employee!" (in fact, do not do that), err on the side of communicating whenever possible: stuff like, "Thanks for following up—I'm swamped with this other thing right now, but I promise I'll get back to you by Thursday."

### Nothing to See Here

Being extra responsive will help you build up some leeway for the times where "home" and "work" collide: for when your Internet suddenly goes out right before a Skype meeting, for when your dryer buzzes while you're on the phone, for when your dog has a colossal accident that needs immediate attention. That stuff's going to happen, and occasionally it might cause real problems, so you want to avoid the perception that it's happening all the time.

Plus, let's be real: unless your position requires you to be on call during specific hours, maybe you *do* want to duck out early to hit the mall occasionally. As long as you're meeting your goals and supporting your coworkers—and, needless to say, being thoughtful and strategic about the times when you go off the grid—that shouldn't be a problem. Whereas if you're constantly dropping offline, or generally half-assing your work, you're likely to find yourself re-tethered to the office (if not out of a job entirely).

### In the Downtime

Realistically, no one spends their *entire* workday in a tornado of productivity, regardless of where they happen to be sitting—but the distractions are different in a home office. You've got all the chores and tasks that are part of the domestic sphere, as opposed to random side conversations with coworkers. It's pretty much a wash in terms of which place is the most inherently work-friendly—assuming you're actually staying focused on work while you're at home.

To keep your productivity up as a remote employee, try to schedule your distractions so that they coincide with the natural ebbs in your workflow. Mindless tasks like folding laundry can be great for resetting your brain when you're stuck on an idea or getting frustrated. You just have to make sure your proportion of downtime isn't bigger than it would've been in the onsite days, and remember that your job should nearly always come first. If you let home maintenance take precedence over sitting down at your desk, your domestic sphere might be a thing of beauty, but you'll find your professional to-do list getting longer—and your stress level, correspondingly higher—with every passing day.

## You Can Clock Out Any Time You Like—But You Can Never Leave

When people act like working from home is the be-all end-all of cushy jobs, I'm . . . confused. Even though I absolutely appreciate the upsides.

Because if you work from home, your home *is* your office. I mean, sure, you can go to a co-working space or whatever, but for most remote employees, the domicile is the default.

When you're office-based, there are times when a work issue pops up on your after-hours e-mail radar and you—blissfully—*can't do anything about it.* Oh, how I miss those days. You don't have that file with you, you don't have the right software program on your personal laptop, you don't have access to the server—all airtight excuses for inaction. Moreover, office-based folks aren't grappling with a remote employee's justifiable concerns about seeming unreliably available. You'll be there in the morning. Your coworkers all know how late you were there last night. It's *fine.* But when you work from home, you're faced with a dilemma: sure, technically you're eating dinner, but you couuuuuuld jump up and grab your laptop. If you're someone who strives for a good work/life balance (and I'd argue you should be), it's a lot harder to enforce those boundaries when work is literally in the next room.

On a practical level, a home office offers no context cues for "time to pack it up" whenever quitting time rolls around. Maybe your pet starts harassing you for dinner or your spouse comes home and expresses concern that you're still working, but you definitely don't have the growing chorus of "well, see you tomorrow!"s that helps usher you out of an onsite workday. And if you have neither partners nor pets to snap you back to non-work reality, you can suddenly look up from your computer screen to see that it's completely dark outside and you've somehow postponed your dinner past 9 P.M.

Now, sometimes the ability to work long into the night can be a benefit—you can plug away at a big project without interruptions, which might even buy you some extra free time later in the week. Still, you have to make sure you're doing that by choice and not by default. If you're finding it hard to formally disengage, get in the habit of watching the clock closely and dramatically closing up the computer whenever you've hit a natural stopping point circa end-of-day. Surely there are other things you could be doing—and if you really can't think of anything, work will always be there.

### Also, It's Not Called "Fun from Home"

Maybe you're not worried about forcibly disconnecting at the end of the day and you're fully capable of remaining in active contact with your colleagues. There's still one final issue with working remotely, which is: you do, in fact, have to work. Except that there's no one there to make you.

Eventually—inevitably—slacking off will catch up with you. But it will take time.

An unscrupulous remote employee could test their manager's oversight by screwing around all day instead of actually working. They might even get away with it too, depending on their role and the other stuff going on at their organization.

But—even though it's important to acknowledge the negatives—work-from-home options are a huge net positive for employees. They're particularly beneficial for workers who have often been sidelined by more traditional schedule models: parents, students, people with disabilities, and artist types whose side gigs interfere with an onsite 9-to-5. Abusing the system ruins it for everyone, and is that really a group you want to be hurting because of your own laziness?

I didn't think so. Now get up off your couch, reread the anti-procrastination section if you have to, and get to work. (Or, if you're the neurotically conscientious type who feels guilty putting their laptop away at the end of the day—A.K.A. My People— consider this your license to go do something fun for a while. You deserve it.)

CHAPTER 5

## YOU'RE ALL IN THIS TOGETHER:
# Dealing with Bosses, Coworkers, and Other Workplace Inhabitants

IT'S EASY TO think of your job as a little bubble, where you sit with the tasks you're responsible for and quietly unleash your productivity onto the world. But there are always going to be other people to contend with. You're going to have a boss, you're going to have coworkers, and you're going to have to navigate your relationships with the cast of characters populating your office. For the employed, interpersonal interaction is unavoidable.

While you might think that the ideal job is one where you're best buddies with all your colleagues, that's not necessarily true. Sometimes you might actively dislike most of your officemates, but love the work enough that you're willing to put up with them. You could have a boss who's a vicious hardass, but who pushes you to accomplish things you never would've thought you were capable of—or you could have a sweet-as-sugar boss who lets you get away with murder. The second one might be more pleasant to deal with, but the first will be better for your long-term personal growth. Even if you're lucky enough to make friends with your coworkers, that can cause its own issues: if you have to choose between a friendship and your own professional integrity, which are you going to pick?

Regardless of the personal dynamics in your particular workplace, you need to find a way to get along reasonably well with everyone. It will require diplomacy, tact, and not saying the first thing that pops into your head, with a few tough choices and moments of awkwardness thrown in for good measure.

This is ultimately a bigger topic than even one chapter can contain: relationships are integral to almost every aspect of your working life. But here, I'm going to focus on the techniques you can use to keep things copacetic with your coworkers. Like anything else about a job, it's a skill—and that doesn't mean you have to be "fake" or insincere. It just means you have to be thoughtful, and if you take that approach from your first day on the job, it will spare you a lot of headaches later on.

# Conflicts and Interests

*Managing fraught work relationships and (politely) holding your colleagues accountable*

Dear Businesslady,

I'm chugging along in my first postcollege job and the work itself is fine, but I was really unprepared for the degree to which personal relationships seem to affect everything my office does. Someone will be randomly rude to me in the hallway, and then it turns out they're overseeing a project I was just assigned to and I have to pretend like we've never met before. Or I'll e-mail someone and then not hear back, and then my boss will be mad that I don't have the info I was asking about—but "so-and-so didn't respond" just sounds like I'm being whiny.

I know that I'm dealing with human beings and not robots, and that sometimes individual personalities are going to come into play. But I just get so frustrated sometimes! Especially since I'm relatively new to the office, it feels like there's this secret code of behavior that everyone knows except me. I'm always worried I'll commit some faux pas or forever change a higher-up's opinion of me because I e-mailed them one too many times.

Is this just a "suck it up and deal" kind of thing, or are there strategies for navigating this weird stew of social dynamics?

—Org Chart vs. Borg Chart

➤ There are always going to be coworkers you can't stand, or just don't understand. You can complain about them all you want on your downtime, but while you're on the clock, keeping things collegial is officially part of your job. Not only is it expected of you (and it definitely is), it's also essential to your success. Even the most independent workers will sometimes need to rely on the kindness of colleagues.

### Every Little Thing They Do Is Maddening

Humanity is a rich tapestry. For every delightful person who imbues your life with joy, there's someone who seems scientifically engineered to aggravate you. Let's go ahead and call these folks the Irritators.

The thing about Irritators is that they're everywhere, but you don't always have the opportunity to realize it. It's only once you're forced into close proximity with them—if they're a member of your family, let's say, or a coworker—that you're able to observe their infuriating habits. So while they might *seem* to disproportionately populate your workplace, that's just an illusion. You might even change jobs just to escape someone who particularly gets under your skin, only to find yourself plagued by an even worse specimen at your next gig.

Plus, every office is going to have its share of people who are stressed, people who are sleep-deprived, people who are quietly trying to manage personal issues, and so on—sometimes, those people will be you. It's an environment almost tailor-made for creating short fuses. Whenever you find yourself getting impatient with a colleague, try to be understanding—that's how you build up karma for the instances when you (yes, even *you*) are someone else's Irritator, purely due to circumstance.

You just have to suffer Irritators with as much cheerfulness as you can muster. Unless they're somehow interfering with your actual work (because they're your boss, because they're actively being malicious, or because there's some other complexity involved—all of which I'll address later in this chapter), focus on whatever good qualities they have and do your best to curtail your irritation.

## Being the Bigger Person

While you're allowed to be extra friendly to people you develop a particular rapport with, there's a certain baseline of politeness that you have to maintain with everybody. You can mentally deride your coworkers' politics or fashion choices or odorific lunchtime meals, but you have to keep those thoughts separate from the part of your brain that controls public conversation and e-mail-writing.

For people who are actively mean, this becomes a bit trickier. Trying to reform the office curmudgeon is probably not a battle worth fighting, especially if they're just That Way and you're not getting singled out. That still doesn't mean you have to sink to their level. At best, snarking back will be a temporary victory that reinforces a poor standard of interpersonal conduct—and at worst, it could get you in trouble with supervisors who don't agree that your snippy tone was warranted. If you're relentlessly pleasant, at least you can be confident that your own behavior is beyond reproach (and maybe, just maybe, your charm offensive will eventually soften them up over time).

## Help Me Help You Help Me

All of this "get along with your coworkers" stuff isn't just about following the rules of professional conduct—it will be crucial when you need to collaborate with people and even more vital if you're asking for a favor. If you're only cordial when you need something, your colleagues will notice that pretty quickly.

While the age-old adage of "if you can't say anything nice, don't say anything at all" is a decent rule for the workplace, sometimes you have no choice but to deliver an unpleasant message. So I think we need a corollary: "if you have to say something not-nice, try to say it nicely."

Let's say you've got a report due to your boss at the end of the day on Friday, and your coworker Tim is responsible for providing you with the charts that you're supposed to include. He swore he'd have them to you on Wednesday, but it's Thursday afternoon and they still haven't materialized yet (. . . ugh, classic Tim).

It'd be tempting to send him an e-mail like "Hey jackass, you want to send me those charts or do you want me to tell Sharon it's your fault that the report's not done?" It'd also be tempting to just send the incomplete report along, copying Tim: "Dear Sharon, Sorry this report doesn't have charts—Tim never finished them." But unless you're planning on leaving the workforce immediately following this project, that's only going to cause problems for you—problems that go far beyond whatever momentary shame you manage to cultivate in poor Tim.

Whenever you have to call out a colleague, you want to do it in a spirit of apologetic collaboration, the kind of "I hate to tell you this" vibe of informing someone about a piece of errant spinach in their teeth. Stick to the facts at hand—don't editorialize about your coworkers' productivity or work habits. It's a manager's job to make sure everyone's pulling their weight. Your job is to just . . . do your job.

So in this example, you e-mail Tim: "Hey, I just wanted to confirm you're still working on those charts—Sharon's expecting the report by Friday, so I need them by lunchtime at the latest if they're going to be included." If you don't get a prompt response that assuages your concerns, try following up a different way—a phone call, IM, or stopping by his desk. If *that* still doesn't work, and it's now Friday morning, then you go to your boss: "Sharon, I'm still hoping to finish up that report on schedule, but I still don't have charts from Tim and I don't know if they'll be available by the deadline. Is it okay if I get you everything by Monday?" She's not an idiot—she can figure out the problem here. But you're not overstepping your boundaries by critiquing anyone's performance, and if the reason for the delay is that Tim got pulled into an even higher-priority project that took up all his chart-making time, you won't be in the position of backpedaling your more aggressive approach.

## Work Means Sometimes Having to Say You're Sorry

Before we move on to more difficult sub-realms of the office social scene, let me leave you with this. As in any relationship, there are going to be times when you inflict a less-than-stellar version of yourself on your coworkers—ill-advisedly pressing Send on an angry e-mail or being cranky when you're caught at a bad moment. That shouldn't be an issue unless it becomes a pattern, and the easiest way to ensure it blows over is by owning up to it like you would any other professional mistake. You don't need to make that big a deal out of it, but you should apologize if it feels like you crossed a line. Blame a lack of food/sleep/caffeine or an overabundance of stress if you're worried about what to say. The goal is to reset back to generalized friendliness and a dynamic of "we treat each other with a certain level of courtesy here."

# I Hate Your Face

*Keeping it together when your boss is a jerk*

Dear Businesslady,

My boss sucks. I'm not looking for advice on how to make her change because I know that's a lost cause. I just need to figure out how to get through the workday without completely losing my mind.

She's terrible at communication, but then gets furious when I misunderstand or misinterpret something she (confusingly) said. She hates being asked questions, hates anything less than the most succinct of statements, and is almost pathologically un-empathetic when my personal life occasionally intrudes into the workplace. (Obviously I'm not trying to chat with her about my hopes and dreams or anything, but as an example, when I needed to get an emergency medical procedure done, her only response was a heavy sigh/eyeroll and then asking when I'd be back.)

I need to stay in this position so that I can keep moving forward in my career, which includes staying on her good side (to the extent that she has one) until I'm ready to move on. Despite her abrasiveness, she's great at what she does and a positive recommendation from her will carry a lot of weight. But I'm starting to feel increasingly unhinged, and I'm afraid I'm going to just yell "SHUT UP!!" at her one day and torpedo everything I've accomplished.

—Serenity Now

➤ If the manager in this letter seems familiar, you too might be working for someone who could use some training in effective mentorship techniques. Or maybe—just maybe—your boss happens to have a different style than yours, or is holding you to a higher standard than you're ready (and/or willing) to meet at this stage of your career. Really, the source of the friction doesn't matter: if you and your manager don't get along, that's going to be unpleasant for you, and it's not a problem with a simple fix (other than the omnipresent nuclear option of finding another job).

Besides, even the most gloriously thoughtful and nurturing supervisors are going to occasionally introduce angst into the lives of their direct reports, so the strategies in this section are going to be useful for everyone eventually—even those lucky enough to escape the worst that the managerial world has to offer.

## Mind (Self) Control

It would be great if every human being got the respect they inherently deserved—in the workplace and in life. Yet for whatever reason, certain people seem incapable of being polite. You can usually do a decent job of ignoring those folks if they're on the periphery of your workplace, but that's not an option if they're your manager. You can *fantasize* about delivering a scathing monologue to your boss and then storming out as the office explodes behind you, but you can't actually *do* that . . . at least, not in the real world, where people live. So as a socially acceptable alternative, I suggest building up a mental shield that protects you from a jerky boss's worst assaults.

Any advice columnist will tell you that you can't control other people's behavior; you can only control how you respond to it. Your outward reaction needs to conform to certain professional norms (the kind of demeanor I described at the end of Chapter 3), but your internal reaction is just as important, and your psyche will thank you if you manage to wrangle that as well.

## Suffer Fools Calmly

The best way to inoculate yourself against self-doubt, depression, and/or rage (i.e., the natural byproducts of weathering negativity) is to find some kind of mantra you can repeat to yourself when things get rough. It could be "This isn't personal," it could be "This job sucks," it could be "I'm doing this for the experience/paycheck"—whatever rings the most true, and whatever feels the most effectively soothing in the moment. (It doesn't necessarily have to be the same phrase every time, either.)

The purpose of this is to reorient your brain away from fixating on your boss's most recent slight. If you've ever been in a fight with someone—and I'm going to go ahead and assume that you have—then you know how easy it is to stew in your own inner monologue of "I can't believe they had the nerve to . . ." and "Anyone would agree that was out of line." I'd argue that that's not super useful in the aftermath of any conflict, but it's especially counterproductive at the office. So try to find your happy place, and refocus your energies on some work-related thing to distract you from the negative emotions.

## Kindness'd!

The corollary to this is a "kill 'em with kindness" approach for the moments when you're not actively reeling from some instance of shittiness. Most tough bosses don't actively *aspire* to make their employees' lives miserable—they're just difficult to please (and often, also, terrible at explaining what they want). You can attempt to curtail your manager's critiques by performing at your very highest level. Take it as a challenge, as a growth opportunity that will surely serve you well when you have a more supportive boss someday. You may never get a compliment from your manager, but you'll know that the absence of active criticism is a positive reflection on your work, and you should congratulate yourself each time you're able to avoid a new onslaught of gripes.

## You Can't Pick Your Boss, but You Can Pick Your Battles

The techniques I just discussed are for run-of-the-mill obnoxiousness. But it's not as though you have to silently suffer at the hands of a wretched boss until and unless you stop working together. You absolutely can and should speak up about truly problematic incidents and patterns (and I'll get into tactics for that in the next chapter).

The only caveat is that you have to be strategic about what issues you raise—along with when and how you raise them. Even the most sympathetic boss is going to grow weary if you're a never-ending source of grievances, and this section is about least sympathetic bosses.

If something really crosses a line—as in, it might eventually be part of some kind of documented complaint—jot down the relevant details while they're fresh in your mind, but then try to put it aside for a while. It's never wise to start a critical discussion while you're still feeling the full flush of rage/embarrassment/whatever, so a cooling-off period will only help your cause in the long run.

The other reason to take a step back is that there's a limit to the number of times you can say "I have a problem." And unfortunately there's no convenient video game counter that keeps track of your remaining complaint points—although (just like health regeneration in a lot of video games) you do regain your expended points after a certain amount of time has elapsed. Still, it's not an exact science, and it's infinitely variable based on your industry, office culture, seniority, relationship with management, and a host of other factors. The only way to get concrete data on your strategic grievance reserves is when you've fully depleted them—and that's not really a point you want to reach.

So budget your critiques, and unleash them when it seems most worthwhile—a calculation that takes into account the likelihood of getting a positive result as well as how strongly you feel about the issue at hand. Otherwise, you might end up going hard on some minor e-mail rudeness and then find yourself stuck without recourse when serious shit goes down a few days later.

## About That Nuclear Option

If you're constantly warring with your boss, at some point you might want to cut your losses and go work for someone who's more your style. So go find a new job! That won't mean you've "lost" or that they've "won." It doesn't make you weak or incompetent. But your best chance of landing a new gig will be via references from your current employer—and even if you put interviewers in touch with a hundred senior coworkers who all love you, at some point the reference-checkers will likely still want to talk to your much-loathed manager. So once you've decided to jump ship, all the previous advice becomes even more relevant. If you mentally check out as soon as your job search begins, you could be hurting your chance to escape.

# How About That Sportball Game?

*Tips for reasonably pleasant workplace socialization
(hint: the answer isn't "alcohol")*

Dear Businesslady,

My first office party is coming up and I'm officially FREAK-ING OUT. Don't get me wrong, I love parties, but the parties I love are ones where I wake up to a series of photos I don't remember participating in, not ones where I'm hearing about homeowner association woes from my boring coworkers.

I know I need to go because everyone makes a big deal out of it and I already stupidly acknowledged that I was free that night. But I'm scared that I'll either get wasted and embarrass myself or else just have the worst time ever (even though everyone else seems to be actually looking forward to this thing). Should I just embrace my party-girl self and resign myself to being the one that everyone laughs about on Monday morning? I'm fine with that, tbh, but I have a feeling it may not be the best strategy professionally speaking.

—Ain't No Party Like an Office Party

➤ There's no need to overcomplicate this: don't get drunk around your coworkers. I say this knowing that in all likelihood you *will* get drunk around your coworkers—probably many times, at many different jobs. But just because something is somewhat inevitable doesn't mean it's a good idea.

If you don't drink, you can safely skip the next few sections—unless you want to be like, "right, not-drinking, still definitely in favor of that practice."

## Will You Still Respect My Contributions in the Morning?

Here are the pros to getting drunk around your coworkers: it gives you something to do at a party, if there's an open bar it will allow you to get your nonexistent money's worth of free booze, and it might end up prompting more "real" conversations with your colleagues than you're likely to have otherwise.

Here are the cons to getting drunk around your coworkers: it might end up prompting more "real" conversations with your colleagues than you're likely to have otherwise, which could—and likely will—entail some serious overshares. (Also, you could throw up, fall down and hurt yourself, or otherwise be embarrassing—whatever Drunk-You typically does when fully unleashed upon the world.)

There are so many things you don't want to know about your coworkers, and so many things that you don't want your coworkers to know about you. Your most egregious violations of the Don't Get Drunk Around Coworkers rule might be accompanied by the memory fogginess that characterizes serious inebriation, but that doesn't actually help: it just means you'll never know exactly *what* you said and did—or (even more cringeworthy) what other people remember.

### Turn Down for Work

I'll acknowledge that you can make some minor imbibing-related mistakes without ruining your entire career forever. But I've never overindulged around coworkers and then been like, "wow, in retrospect, that was a great idea!" Whatever your usual speed of drinking is, dial it down at least a few notches at work events—especially when you're more junior or otherwise new to an office, and thus more susceptible to being forever branded as The Drunky.

Strive to maintain a level of sobriety where you'd feel comfortable operating a motor vehicle (assuming you're licensed to do so in general, obviously), and make sure you're never the drunkest person in the room by a long shot. If you're just thirsty or need something to do with your hands, the bar should be stocked with plenty of nonalcoholic drinks—the kind that have no effect on your propensity to make bad decisions. (And if all they have is booze, maybe have a word with the party planners about not sabotaging their colleagues' efforts to remain work-appropriate.)

### Why Can't We Be Friends?

You might be thinking there's no hope of cutting loose with your coworkers if you can't throw back a half-dozen drinks. But I'm not saying that you have to spend all night nursing a single glass of wine and blandly discussing the weather, either. I've been lucky enough to form real and lasting friendships with people who started out as "work friends," and at some point those kinds of more intimate relationships allow you to let your guard down.

The problem with booze is that it has a way of short-circuiting your judgment on how *much* guard to let down, and when, and with whom. Not to ruin the magic of How Friends Get Made, but—even with alcohol out of the equation entirely—friendships get forged when one person says something revealing, and the response indicates a meeting of the minds. Then the process repeats itself. You don't just crack a joke one day, hear laughter from the next cubicle, and get matching BFF tattoos on the way home. A solid friendship (even beyond the workplace but especially within one) requires mutual trust, and that takes time to develop.

If you're launching right into raunchy humor and stories of questionable activities with coworkers you don't know that well, it could backfire—particularly if you've misjudged their laughing *at* you as laughing *with* you. Not everyone in your office is your ally, so don't pointlessly provide people with ammo they can fire your way.

## We All Have Stories

At the end of the day (both metaphorically and literally), you'll figure out which colleagues you really click with and those friendships will naturally evolve. But what about the people who are clearly not friend material? You're always going to have coworkers who don't like the same things that you do—and you're still going to have to see and interact with them on the regular.

In a purely social environment, you could probably just write these folks off as "not my style." But an office is about more than that. Your colleagues can be sources of information, of camaraderie, of assistance when you're swamped, and—after you've left that organization and forevermore throughout your career—they're also networking connections. If you find a way to develop some kind of fondness for them, it's a good thing all around.

Plus, you know who's a great source of interesting little anecdotes? Someone whose life differs dramatically from your own. You may *think* you don't care about calf-roping or macramé or cosplay, but if that's your coworker's jam, why not see it as a learning opportunity? Broaden your horizons a bit, and appreciate the chance to gain some insight into the vast diversity of life experiences. If the endgame is going home and telling your partner "Claude got another creepy porcelain doll over the weekend," so be it—as long as you're keeping things friendly at the office.

## Small Talk, Big Rewards

After you've shown yourself to be a good conversationalist, all but the most self-involved of your coworkers will eventually give *you* a turn to gab, which is also good practice for engaging a wide spectrum of the human population. The professional world is full of moments when you have to chitchat with strangers or people you barely know (interviewers, fellow conference attendees, randos in the same elevator, etc.), and having a stockpile of work-appropriate stories makes those moments more enjoyable for everyone. The ability to break an awkward silence is a real gift, and if you generate an authentic chuckle in the process, you'll have genuinely brightened the mood of everyone around you. It also might be your opening to start a longer conversation with a new person—and you never know, maybe they'll be able to offer you some career help down the line. Small talk is a skill like any other, so don't miss the opportunity to cultivate it.

# On Wednesdays We Wear Pink Slips

*Negotiating office cliques*

Dear Businesslady,

Thanks to a promotion (yay!) and an office relocation (y . . . ay?) I'm in a completely different spot than how I've spent the majority of my fledgling career. I'm already a little isolated based on my job description, and everyone else on my team is pretty tight-knit—lots of inside jokes and references that sail right over my head.

So, that part's pretty normal I guess. But lately there have been some other things that feel a little . . . meaner. I've walked in on hushed conversations that abruptly stopped when someone noticed me, and a few times there've been weird bouts of simultaneous giggling that coincided with something I did. Maybe I'm being paranoid, but also, maybe I'm being secretly made fun of, right?

Most recently, I was totally left out of a meeting with our boss and another unit regarding a major team project. It was supposedly an accident—and to be fair, the organizer did apologize profusely—but with all this other stuff I can't help but wonder.

I'm not really sure how to handle it, because all these isolated incidents seem minor on their own, and it's hard to aggregate them without sounding like I'm obsessing. But it's starting to wear on me. Should I say something? And to who—them? Our boss? HR? I don't even care if they don't like me, particularly, but I need to be able to work with them.

—Not Here to Make Friends (Apparently)

➡ UGH, THIS SUCKS. It sucks to be excluded, it sucks to feel (know?) that you're the butt of other people's mean-spirited jokes, and—most importantly—it sucks to worry that other people's juvenile nonsense is going to affect your career.

If someone wrote to me complaining about "ugh, this new coworker is soooo uncool and she ruins the vibe of our office girl squad—it's okay to treat her like crap, right?" I would respond, "of course not—are you a fucking *child?!*" But even though I'd love to unleash my fury on a bully, I don't really have any suggestions for How to Develop Some Empathy—whereas I do have advice for anyone unfortunate enough to be on the receiving end of this kind of treatment.

### Stop Trying to Make Fetch Happen

It doesn't matter whether you're the target of an aggressive exclusion campaign or just misreading the degree to which you're simpatico with another person—either way, it's not possible to make other people like you. Even if they eventually change their minds and you do become friends, that's going to happen organically, not because you finally cracked the secret code to their affections.

So step one in a scenario like this is: accept that these people aren't your friends, assume that they never will be, and don't try to ingratiate yourself. You should still be polite to them, though, because that's how grown-ups treat their coworkers. And if they're actively being obnoxious, you have my permission to imbue your pleasantries with a note of chilliness—as long as you keep it subtle enough that it doesn't qualify as stooping to their level.

### The Limit Does Exist

It's one thing to work alongside people who are closer with each other than they are with you—it's not necessarily fun, but it's manageable. That changes if it starts to impact your actual job.

Even if no one's deliberately trying to slight you, your coworkers' insularity could diminish your professional prospects. Maybe there's unconscious favoritism on the part of someone with decision-making power, or a lot of important brainstorming ends up happening at informal in-crowd gatherings that aren't official work events.

Everyone becomes part of a subgroup at some point—regardless of whether you're purposely trying to exclude anyone—and even the most innocuous cliques could have serious consequences. This is why it's crucial to constantly check yourself for unintentional bias. More insidious kinds of sidelining often coincide with straight-up racism, sexism, or other despicable "us vs. your kind" behaviors—even if no one involved is actively thinking, "Let's not invite the Muslim guy to bowling night" and then rubbing their hands together like a cartoon villain. Dismissing that stuff as though it's only relevant to the social side of things is how actual problems are allowed to persist.

### Your "How I've Been Burned" Book

If being outside of your office's inner circle is affecting your work, then you need to take action. The exact tactics will depend on the particulars of your problem, and I'll go over an array of "tough conversations" techniques in the next chapter. But first, start keeping a private log where you track the ways in which you've been affected. It's not easy to correct stuff like this, and sadly that means there's an incentive for management to dismiss your complaint as an isolated incident. Your organization's leadership is much more likely (and in many instances, legally obligated) to act if you can demonstrate a clear pattern.

As you're documenting things, keep in mind that you might be asked to hand over your notes as reference material while the higher-ups figure out how to address the issue. It's not going to help your case if you list petty and inconsequential slights amid the more serious offenses, nor is it productive to editorialize.

What you want in terms of Official Documentation is something impassive, factual, and outcomes-focused. Like: "This was the third time someone else was given the opportunity to present our team's project to the CEO, even though I have seniority and specifically requested to be involved. My manager didn't offer an explanation for selecting others over me but confirmed that my performance was not an issue. I'm concerned that my work isn't enjoying the same level of visibility as my colleagues." You might be tempted to add "Of course she let her buddy *Gretchen* present, even though she's a terrible public speaker and her PowerPoint was littered with typos," but save that commentary for your conversations with friends or your diary.

### This New Thing Where You Don't Talk About People Behind Their Backs

Once you've gathered your ammunition, the next step is *not* contacting someone with authority over the culprits. You might be completely certain that your tormentor(s) won't change their behavior, but you still need to raise the problem with them directly before escalating it, for a few reasons: (1) On the off chance that they're totally innocent and appalled upon realizing what they've been doing, it's the quickest, simplest, and kindest way to fix things. (2) It prevents them from pulling any kind of "oh but I had *no idea*, I wish you had *said something*" crap whenever they're asked to account for themselves. And (3) some version of "I told them but the issues continued" is an especially powerful detail to include in your documentation.

### She Doesn't Even Go Here (Anymore)

Unless your workplace is just one giant clique plus you, the problem should be corrected once you bring it to the right people's attention. Still, if you're working under indifferent/incompetent managers, or facing an especially sneaky and nasty cadre of cool kids, there's a chance that nothing will change. Or maybe the official work-related issues get addressed but they're accompanied by a heightened vibe of We Don't Like You and We Wish You Weren't Here. In that case, it's time to bust out that old standard—sing it with me, folks!—finding a new job. Better to start over somewhere else than to let the life-ruiners of the world ruin your life—or at least, your weekdays.

# Since You've Been Gone

*Dealing with departures and their effects on productivity and morale*

Dear Businesslady,

A year or two ago, if you'd asked if I liked my job, I would've answered, "I love it." I was part of a great team that worked together beautifully.

Then the layoffs started. We lost a bunch of long-standing employees—the kind of people who knew *everything* and were like the office moms—and then a few more people found new jobs because they were worried about where things were going.

Now, stuff's stabilized and we've all been assured that no one else is gonna be let go. But it's really hard to get anything done these days. We've hired a couple replacement people who don't really "get it," and I can tell they're getting annoyed with our constant references to people who aren't here anymore.

I know we should all be working harder than ever to make sure revenue stays high, but it's tough to feel motivated. The office feels like a ghost town, and there's a general sense of "what's the point"—I know I'm not the only one feeling it. My new boss is trying super hard to bring us together, but all I can think about is how my old boss would've handled things, and then I just get sad. And then I feel dumb for feeling sad, because it's just work, right?

I'd consider leaving, but I don't want to make things worse for the few long-term people who are still here—and despite all this, I still enjoy the work I do. I just want to like my job again, and I don't know if things will ever be the same.

—The Last Unicorn

An office represents a delicate ecosystem, interdependent in ways that aren't always easy to see. You may think your job is entirely separate from the world inhabited by your coworkers—until one of them leaves and there's a palpable sense of loss.

And when you lose a bunch of people at once—which usually, in one way or another, indicates some kind of corresponding instability within the organization itself—it can truly feel like you're working in the aftermath of the apocalypse.

### It's the End of the World as We Know It

Mass departures—A.K.A. (almost always) layoffs—take the problem of a single absent colleague and magnify it, sometimes enormously. Layoffs are a bummer while they're happening—even though there are plenty of companies that reduce their staff, fix whatever their financial/managerial problems were, and then go on to great success. It's like losing your wallet: you'll eventually be okay, but only after enduring a period of significant unpleasantness. (Those who actually get laid off are in a similar spot—it's anxiety-inducing to find yourself suddenly out of work, even if it might ultimately lead to a new and amazing job.)

It's natural to really *feel* this sense of unease, and you should let yourself feel it. Have you ever successfully bottled up an emotion—repressed it entirely out of existence? Me neither. The longer you try to pretend everything is fine, the longer you'll be plagued by a vague feeling of worry—and worry is antithetical to productivity. You can't do your best work while there's a voice in your head going, "Like this even *matters*, will any of us even *be* here a year from now?" So allow yourself to freak out for a while about the significant changes that surround you—and then try to shake it off so that you can start moving forward.

### . . . And I Feel Fine

There's something apocalyptic about a time of transition, true. But then again, we live in a culture replete with triumphant post-apocalyptic narratives. We love the idea of rising from the ashes, achieving great things in the face of tremendous challenges.

While your ability to pull off a conference despite missing a few team members might not make you Furiosa from the *Mad Max* universe, it's a victory nonetheless.

Every organization has a certain "how we've always done things" inertia, and a shakeup in your routines can shake loose new ideas that actually make things better. When you're forced to make tough decisions, you look at everything more critically—making do with less means figuring out where your priorities lie. It can be a real opportunity . . . *but*, you have to be willing to see it that way.

### Embrace the Changes
Remaining focused on the way things were will prevent you from adjusting to your new reality. In addition to keeping you stuck in a bad mental spot, it will put a little cloud of negativity around you that can take its toll on your coworkers. This can be especially toxic if your organization is still bringing on new people—who wants to start a new job in an office that's steeped in defeatist pessimism and embittered nostalgia?

Instead, to whatever extent your role and personal temperament allow, try to rally your colleagues. Those "triumph over adversity" stories are always about people banding together—a movie about people listlessly complaining to one another is going to tank at the box office. Take it upon yourself to find solutions for whatever issues your team is dealing with, and consider it part of your job duties to make a positive impact on morale. That attitude will eventually start to rub off on other people, and soon you'll all feel that the worst times are now behind you.

### Be the Change You Wish to See in the Workplace
Whether you've lost a large group or just one person, there's always a void when someone leaves an office. Now, granted, sometimes that void might be accompanied by a sense of celebration or relief (if the departing coworker was a total slacker and/or profoundly disagreeable to be around), but most of the time, you miss your colleagues once they're gone. Even someone you never

connected with on a personal level could have a particular way of doing things, or of making sure things get done, that makes them surprisingly irreplaceable. Still, though, you can't change things back to how they used to be through sheer force of will. So if you're missing some aspect of the old era, try to figure out how to re-create it in your present circumstances. Maybe you need to spend some time getting to know the "new guy" so you feel the same camaraderie you did with his predecessor. Maybe you need to suggest a new workflow that makes the most of your team's individual skills. Or maybe you need to identify what made your former coworker so indispensable and then incorporate those same qualities into your own style.

### That Was Then, This Is Now

The reality is, people leave jobs all the time. Even layoffs, as dramatic and disruptive as they are when you're experiencing them, aren't terribly uncommon throughout the working world. So while your initial reaction might be "I can't believe this is happening," you need to get to a point of acceptance as quickly as possible. Like any major change, once you get far enough beyond it, you'll be able to look back with some perspective—and you'll see that, while you might miss certain things about the past, there are good things about the present that would never have happened otherwise.

# The Coworkers Who Knew Too Much

*Keeping workplace friendships professional—*
*and moving on if (when?) things go sour*

Dear Businesslady,

A few years ago, one of my college friends founded a startup and hired me to handle payroll—mainly because I needed a job and she wanted me to move out to California with her. For a while, life as the CEO's buddy was pretty sweet: I got the inside scoop on everything, a cushy office, and lots of other little perks. I didn't always agree with her business decisions, but I respected her authority and kept my mouth shut.

Our finances started getting shakier, though, and eventually we needed a bigger org to buy us out in order to stay afloat. Now we're part of this new corporate structure, and everything's gotten real problematic.

My friend is still here, and still senior to me, but we report to the same person. I'm actually happy with how things worked out, because I've acquired some additional duties that I'm genuinely excited about. But she is emphatically NOT happy and takes every opportunity to sigh about how much better life was when she was in charge. Her former employees still see her as the de facto leader, so it's causing a lot of tension with our actual boss. As much as I still love and value her as a friend, I don't necessarily want to be associated with Team Her whenever this all comes to a head.

I tried to talk to her about this, but she flipped out, implying I was being disloyal and siding with our corporate overlords. That seems like an oversimplification, but whatever—now I'm just hoping I don't have to choose between my friend and my career. Do I?

—Chief Frenemy Officer

➤ Having a close friend at your job is a lot like getting drunk around your coworkers: not a great idea, but something that happens regardless. Even if you try to keep your personal and professional lives distinct, you never know when you'll bond with one of your colleagues, and it's hard to turn down the rare opportunity to make a new friend. Nevertheless, you should know from the outset that it might complicate your working life, and plan accordingly.

### Whose Side Are You On, Anyway?

The problems with office friendships all circulate around one main theme: what happens when there's a conflict between a relationship you value and your professional best interests.

If the friendship dissolves or otherwise drifts apart, that can be awkward, sure—maybe even unpleasant. But at least that situation comes equipped with clear priorities: your job first, your kinda-sorta-ex-friend a distant second.

It's much more difficult when your duties as a friend and as an employee are in direct opposition to one another. If your buddy has a major beef with management, are you going to join the fight or remain on the sidelines? If your friend engages in unscrupulous or otherwise shady behavior, and your boss asks about it, what will you say? If you're given the chance at a promotion that would put you above your friend in the chain of command—requiring you to put the friendship on pause for as long as you're in a manager/direct-report relationship—will you take the opportunity?

To be clear, I'm not trying to suggest that your job should always take precedence over your friendships. Work is only one component of a rich and fulfilling life, and you're perfectly within your rights to sacrifice your professional advancement (which is the worst-case scenario here) in order to preserve a friendship that you value.

It's just that you need to have your priorities in line as soon as you realize there's a potential for trouble. If you're blindsided by the need to choose between your friend and work, you might act without thinking—siding with your manager even though they're clearly in the wrong, or banding together with your coworker-friend even though it will damage relations with your boss. It's one thing to face the consequences after taking a considered, principled stand, whereas dealing with fallout from a knee-jerk decision can make everything that follows feel profoundly unfair.

## Take It Slow

Because so much can go wrong when you're friends with a colleague, it's wise to be cautious when developing closer relationships with your coworkers. I mean, think about your friends—the ones you didn't meet at the office. No matter how tight you are, how much do you know about their workplace personas? Do you know what kind of colleagues they are, what their productivity is like, how good they are with deadlines? My guess is, probably not. With your extracurricular friendships, those things don't really matter.

If you work together, though, those things *do* matter. Your reputation is one of your most powerful professional resources, and you cultivate and protect it by demonstrating consistent good judgment. When you form an office friendship, it's usually pretty obvious to those around you—and if that friendship means allying yourself with a low performer, it's likely to affect others' perceptions of your own work ethic.

It's also challenging to put a burgeoning friendship on the back burner once a pattern has been established. If you occasionally have lunch with someone, but sometimes eat at your desk, you can probably curtail the lunches entirely without having a big discussion about it. Whereas if you have a standing happy-hour date every Friday with a particular friend, you can't just stop showing up without explaining yourself.

So as you start developing affinities for particular coworkers, be cautious about escalating things into full-blown friendships. At the same time, be on the lookout for any foreshadowing of future issues. A predisposition toward things like grudge-holding, gleeful rule-breaking, dishonesty (however benign), or flagrantly risqué jokes can often be a warning sign that a Them vs. Your Reputation reckoning is on the horizon. Again, it's up to you whether or not you want to take that risk—but if that reckoning comes, you want to be ready for it.

### It's Not You, It's Work

There are enough hypothetical job + friend combinations out there to make this situation nearly impossible to consider in the abstract. On the one hand, the idea of pursuing professional success at the expense of interpersonal relationships sounds way too Machiavellian for my taste. Plus, I've been in the position of sticking up for a wronged friend—voicing my concerns, emphatically, to management—and even if it wasn't the greatest decision professionally, it felt really good emotionally. I'd do it again.

On the other hand, there actually isn't an infinite pool of jobs out there—at least not well-paying, reasonably enjoyable jobs that align with your long-term goals. And if we're talking about the type of priceless friend who's worth keeping in your life indefinitely, isn't that person also more likely to be understanding when you need to make a tough choice?

Bottom line, if irreconcilable differences arise between your career aspirations and the continuation of a workplace friendship, you may have to have some version of the break-up conversation. The difference here is that instead of "I hope we can still be friends" you're saying "I hope that someday—when our jobs aren't directly impacted by our friendship—we can pick up where we left off." (Or maybe you're saying, "I used to think you were cool but now I realize you're incredibly irresponsible, so good luck with that and peace out." Either way, it's A Talk.)

### You Gotta Keep 'Em Separated

Whether preemptively or after some kind of official downgrade in friendship status, it's best if you keep your social life and your professional life as mutually exclusive as possible. You can be friend-*ly* with people above or below you in the managerial hierarchy, but you can't be actual, hang-out-outside-of-work friends. Period.

Peer friendships are a bit more permissible, although if you're inseparable and constantly cracking inside jokes around the office, your other colleagues might accuse you of cliquishness or favoritism—regardless of whether or not you're actually guilty.

Also, it can make your life more difficult to have your coworkers all up in your business. When you're trying to get out of an after-hours meeting, "I have another commitment" is much more compelling when there's no one to pipe up with "What, your weekly bar trivia game? C'mon." Or what about when your work friend asks for help on an assignment you don't want to deal with—"I'm super swamped right now" won't work if they know you spent most of the day on a massive online-shopping quest.

If my experience is any indication, the best—and most worthwhile—work friendships develop regardless of your best efforts to cordon off your personal life. If you're keeping your boundaries firm and remaining focused on doing a good job, you're much less likely to become entangled with problematic rogue actors, but you *will* fall in with like-minded people who appreciate your work ethic as much as your sense of humor. And when one or the other of you decamps for a new position, then all of those concerns go away entirely: they just become one more friend that you're lucky to have, and the fact that you met at work is ancient history.

## CHAPTER 6

# Tackling Tricky Topics with Grace and Aplomb

NO MATTER HOW great your job is, eventually you're going to run into a situation that demands a difficult discussion—and a delicate touch. Whether it's a serious complaint, a personal issue with professional ramifications, or some potentially touchy feedback, these are the kinds of conversations that require careful forethought and (usually) meticulous preparation. If you approach them too casually, you run the risk of undermining whatever outcome you hoped to achieve.

You might be tempted to avoid these talks entirely, but silence is a terrible way of effecting change (and sometimes not even an option). Instead of avoidance, it's better to find small-scale ways to practice tackling thorny topics. If you get comfortable with speaking up, voicing an unpopular opinion, and advocating for yourself in general, you'll be better equipped to rise to the occasion whenever the stakes are high.

There isn't a set of magic words that prevents tough conversations from being, well, tough. And sadly, there's also no way to ensure that you'll get the results you were hoping for—even the most well-reasoned arguments can be useless against unreasonable people.

However, there are techniques you can use to help make fraught discussions go more smoothly: to minimize awkwardness, tension, and defensiveness for everyone involved. If you deploy these, you'll increase your chances of success—and, if things don't go your way, you'll at least have the comfort of knowing that you did everything you could.

It's a real bummer to walk away from an important conversation with the feeling that you went about it all wrong, and I'm here to prevent that from happening.

# Use Your Words

*Initiating difficult conversations with
your boss or coworkers*

Dear Businesslady,

My organization has been going through a lot of ch-ch-changes lately and the result is a corresponding downturn in my job satisfaction. I'm a generally easygoing person and I know my boss has been overwhelmed with trying to adapt to the new structure, so I've just been going with the flow with the perspective of "I'll see how I feel once the dust has settled."

Well, now that dust is settling, and I find myself actively annoyed, frustrated, or baffled on a daily basis. I feel like I owe it to my boss to voice my objections and see if there's any hope of shifting things around so that I'm happier—the problem is HOW to have that conversation. It's this muddy mix of personal frustrations, big-picture stuff about the org, issues with coworkers and workflow, and then a bunch of one-off random things.

I know I can't just info-dump like "I don't think Jerry has been doing a good job handling tech support AND ALSO my new chair is uncomfortable" but it all feels equally important. When I finally take a deep breath and start launching into this discussion, what should come out?

—Untie My Tongue

➤ "Yay, a tough conversation!"—said no one ever. Yet difficult discussions are inevitable, so you can either blunder your way through them or use them as an opportunity to fix otherwise intractable problems. This section is a general primer for the trickiest of real talk—specifically with managers, although most of it is applicable to coworkers as well. Let's start with the basics.

### Organize Your Thoughts

Before you open your mouth, you need to be prepared. Personally, I like to write down a list of everything that's on my mind regarding the topic at hand—from the really important stuff that must be addressed all the way down to the petty asides that shouldn't even be brought up. Seeing it all in one place helps me decide how to categorize it, and eventually a rough hierarchy will emerge: one main point, a few secondary issues, and then a slew of things that I'll only mention if they end up becoming relevant.

With your prep work done, you can transfer your findings to a separate list—one you won't be embarrassed about if your manager happens to see it in the course of the discussion. For the letterwriter's scenario, it might look something like this:

- Productivity (workflow, assignment of duties across colleagues)
- Resources (desk equipment, tech support)
- Miscellaneous (job satisfaction, organizational structure)

You never know how these sorts of discussions will go—sometimes it's "thanks for raising this; tell me more," and other times it's "your concerns are noted; good day." So you want to lead with your highest priority (which means first knowing what that priority *is*) and then take it from there. Otherwise, you might leave your boss's office and realize you ranted for twenty minutes about the copier being janky without ever mentioning that you're desperate to be included on some new projects.

Depending on the issue, this preliminary organization might also include the kind of documentation I mentioned in Chapter 5's "cliques" section. In that case, you'd pull a few key examples that illustrate the pattern you're trying to establish without going into too much granular detail about every single time a version of Event X occurred. (That kind of specificity could prove useful if your manager needs backup for a formal investigation or reprimand, but at this stage it would be overkill and might interfere with your main point—wait until you're asked to provide it.)

## Is Now a Good Time?

Once you've resolved to Bring Shit Up, you might feel compelled to sit down with your manager as soon as you've gotten your thoughts in order—and sure, in theory it's better to minimize the amount of time you spend vibrating with anticipation over this impending conversation. But your moment of motivation might not coincide with an opening in your boss's schedule. If you start the discussion at a disadvantage (by foisting it on someone who's busy, stressed, distracted, or some combination of the three), you'll work against your own interests.

Therefore, the first step of the talk itself is asking permission to have it. You don't need to be weird and cagey about it—"I would like to discuss a MYSTERY TOPIC at your earliest possible convenience" is just silly—but you want to be careful not to describe things in a way that will raise alarm bells. So go with something neutral, but descriptive: "I was wondering if you might have time to talk through some big-picture issues relating to my job" is better than "I must speak with you regarding grave concerns about my future with this company" even if ultimately they describe the same situation. It's a courtesy to warn your manager that a major discussion is on the horizon, but you don't want to worry them unnecessarily.

When you ask "is now a good time," you have to be willing to take "no" for an answer—but that doesn't mean your boss gets to postpone the conversation indefinitely. Feel free to follow up after a respectful amount of time has elapsed (while also remaining sensitive to whatever timing issues were cited during your initial approach, like "after the budgets are in" or whatever). It's okay to get increasingly insistent if the "not now" reasons seem sketchy or you otherwise feel like you're getting the brush-off—but you don't want to start this conversation on an adversarial note, so don't get pissy about the delay. Just keep asking until your moment arrives.

### Framing vs. Blaming

Once the discussion is finally underway, make sure you're approaching things with the right attitude and framing. Even if the reality is that your entire department is in disarray and it's all your manager's fault, that argument isn't likely to generate a favorable response. Your perspective should be collaborative, one of "there's a problem—let's fix it together." Ignore everything your English teacher said about eschewing the passive voice (just this once!) and raise individual issues without addressing causality: "processes are disorganized," "assignments are distributed unfairly," "cellphone noise is distracting," and so on—omit the who, how, and why to whatever extent you can.

### Active Listening

Throughout a meeting like this, your most important job is to **pay attention**. You know what you want to say, and you might even think you know how your manager will respond. You *don't* know exactly how the discussion will unfold, and if you're not listening closely you might miss opportunities to strengthen your case.

Take notes on the points that your boss raises, and adapt your own argument to the direction the conversation is taking. If they offer counterexamples, objections, or explanations, make sure you're really hearing them and that they know they're being heard. Don't just blow past them en route to the next item on your list, or—again—you'll undermine your own authority.

### Lather, Rinse, Repeat

That first discussion may yield tangible results—or it may not. You might get way more pushback than you anticipated, your boss might present counterpoints that totally reorient your perspective, or the meeting might get interrupted by an urgent phone call before it can really get going. So instead of thinking of this as your one shot, think of it as part of an ongoing process.

If the talk is cut short, be assertive in rescheduling it as soon as possible. And with any scenario besides "yes, you're right, here's how we're going to address this," try to come to some kind of agreement regarding next steps. Concluding with "I'll think about the points you raised and let you know if I have any future concerns" serves as a gentle signal that there might be a follow-up conversation. If any promises are made, summarize them before you head out, including a timeline for implementation—and plan to check in with your manager if nothing actually changes.

Finally, always end this kind of discussion by thanking your manager for their time. While it may have been a frustrating experience—full of excuses and "no that's impossible"s from your boss and no meaningful actions on the horizon—you at least got to express yourself, which is something. Plus, a sincere expression of gratitude helps smooth away the uncomfortable "we're in a fight!" vibe that can surround tough conversations. You wanted to talk, you talked, you're grateful you were given the chance to talk—The End, roll credits.

# Um, Actually . . .

*Correcting misunderstandings that have the potential to impact your reputation*

Dear Businesslady,

I've been working my way up the org chart at a medium-sized nonprofit, and I'm hoping to continue building my career here. I really believe in their mission, and the people are great (for the most part—more on that in a sec). Even though there are several layers of hierarchy between us, I've got a good rapport with the executive director, and I think that's why I've managed to move up the ranks so quickly.

My most recent promotion shuffled me over to a new team, with a boss who's fairly new to the organization. He's a nice enough person, but he seems to be really struggling in the role—no one ever knows what they're supposed to be doing and on the rare occasions we do get direct instructions, they're often confusing or outright wrong. This has been frustrating, but I've been trying to ignore it and hope it gets better as he acclimates—and now I'm worried I should've voiced my concerns sooner.

For months we've been working on info packets for potential donors; I was developing the language and working with a freelance team on layout. I thought everything was going well, but I just got a freaked-out e-mail from our executive director because apparently we're three weeks behind deadline (I thought we had another month) and several thousand dollars over budget (I was given a different number). The misinformation, of course, came from my boss—but he gave me the due date and price point during a face-to-face meeting so I have no documentation except my handwritten notes. And our ED thinks this is entirely my fault. Her note ended with "I have to say, this is disappointing and so very unlike you."

I have to say something to clear my name, and probably point out that this isn't the first time our boss has dropped the ball. But how? It's my word against his, and I'm afraid that if I bring up the other issues it'll just seem like I'm whining—or, worse, that I was negligent in keeping silent until now. Should I just grit my teeth and take the blame, hoping this doesn't happen again?

—There's Only Room for One of Us Under This Bus

➡️ I'm getting secondhand anxiety just imagining this situation, because "someone else's screwup is being blamed on me" is such a difficult spot to be in. If you say nothing, you're taking the fall for someone else's mistake—but if you speak up, you risk seeming petty or even dishonest. So you have to proceed with extreme caution.

### Discredit Where Discredit Is Due

It's almost never a good idea to just silently accept blame for something that isn't actually your fault. There are exceptions to every rule, but here are the only circumstances I can think of where it's a reasonable strategy:

1. It's such a minor issue that no one actually cares. This only applies if the supervisors or other stakeholders involved are pretty blasé about it, and if it's an isolated incident (not the latest mistake by someone whose work is generally shoddy). If it feels like you'll just confuse things further by trying to explain—that it'll involve a level of detail that the situation doesn't warrant—then you can hold off.
2. You want to do a favor for the mistake-maker—*and* it's a relatively small error. If it's a colleague who's recently done you a solid, or someone with more to lose (an up-and-coming junior person who doesn't have a great relationship with their boss, for instance), then you can keep quiet. HOWEVER, be careful about this one, because you don't want to be covering up someone's chronic poor performance.

Notice that there's no "#3) To be nice" or "#4) To avoid having a tough conversation." Being forthcoming about process problems doesn't make you a tattletale or a jerk—it makes you a forthright professional who recognizes when an organization isn't functioning properly. Managers need to know if someone's not pulling their weight—they can't do their jobs if they're misinformed about who needs discipline or extra coaching. So if you decide to keep your mouth shut when accused of someone else's error, make absolutely sure you're doing it for one of the two reasons I mentioned earlier, and not out of a misplaced sense of responsibility for other people's mistakes.

### The Truth Will Set You Free

Let's start by assuming that none of your coworkers are outright liars. Realistically that might not always be the case, but I want to believe that most people are fundamentally honest—and more importantly, universal benefit-of-the-doubt is the best approach strategically. If someone's a crook, that'll become apparent eventually, and you can watch it happen from your position on the high road.

The next step is following up with the right people. Who those people are will depend on your role, your relationships with your coworkers, and the nature of the mistake.

If you've been implicated in writing, then you want to make sure the truth gets documented as well. In some cases—with coworkers you know have integrity—you might even forward the original message to them with a note like, "Billy seems to think I messed up the sales projections, but didn't your team work on that?" A good colleague will probably jump into the conversation to clear your name, but not everyone will take the hint. (Keep this in mind whenever you're the one in the wrong—reliably taking responsibility for your own mistakes will prove that you're trustworthy.)

With less dependable actors in the mix, you'll have to do the dirty work yourself—but as with any of these delicate situations, you want to be as dispassionate as possible. You might suspect there was some creative license involved with someone else's explanation, but don't imply that anyone was being intentionally misleading. Just stick to the facts: "Hi all, I just wanted to clear up the workflow on this project since there seems to be some confusion. The sales projections actually came from Tina's team, so hopefully she can explain the inaccuracies." And then you copy Tina on the reply.

Basically, the maneuver here is to *pretend* like your reputation isn't at stake, in spite of how you really feel. If someone told you "New York, NY, is on the West Coast of the United States," you wouldn't get all *how dare you*—you'd just correct them based on the factual reality of the world we all live in. That's the tone you're going for here as well: a kind of bemused vibe of, "I'm not sure why you got this wrong, but no worries—let's clear it up once and for all."

## Calling for Backup

For complex or super-serious situations, it might be wise to enlist your manager as your ally (or another senior colleague who knows the whole story, if the accusation originates with your own boss). If the screwup involves a lot of people—or one particular person who's known to be especially prickly—then a supervisor can help get to the bottom of things. An informal (face-to-face or phone) conversation is probably best, although e-mail will work if necessary. As always, be calm and factual—and as succinct as possible—as you lay out the details and then solicit advice on how to handle it. Even if your boss tells you to deal with it yourself, that preliminary discussion will prove invaluable if things escalate.

## Nuh-Uh! / Yuh-Huh!

Documentation can save your hide in these situations, but if the mistake originates in the course of verbal conversation, the only official evidence will be highly fallible human memory. Someone still has to back down, though—and sometimes, for whatever reason, that person is going to have to be you. But that doesn't mean you have to admit outright defeat. In the same neutral "mistakes were made" tone as in all these other examples, you can issue a verdict of "well, I remember it differently, but what's done is done, and I suppose this is a lesson to take better notes." (And then, needless to say, you *do* start keeping a more robust record so that you don't find yourself in this position again.)

Sometimes when a big project goes awry, there's no clear target for blame and so it just kind of splashes all over everyone involved.

If that happens—or you otherwise get dinged for something you really couldn't control—try not to let it get to you. A crusade to indict the real culprit isn't a good look. If your work is otherwise good, and you've proven yourself to be an upright citizen in the office, your reputation can safely survive a few mistakes . . . even the ones that aren't actually yours.

# Your Mother Doesn't Work Here (And Even If She Did . . .)

*Addressing and overcoming sexism*

Dear Businesslady,

I have a workplace gripe that I'm hesitant to call "sexism" if it's really just obliviousness—and at the same time, I feel dumb calling out "sexism" when it's not like I'm being actively denied a promotion because someone thinks I'm a dumb emotional woman. And beyond all that, I'm just really irritated and need help dealing with that in a more constructive way than just sitting and seething. (Also, I know this is long, but it's complicated and I want to make sure you have all the details.)

So, tell me if I'm over- or under-reacting. I'm an accountant in one department of a ginormous company, and once a month(ish) all the accountants, from all departments, get together for a lunch meeting. We "share best practices" (she said, corporately) and get to know new hires and so on. It's a good program and I'd hate to give it up, since I've learned a lot from this group.

But. The lunches are always organized by this one guy who's been there longer than anyone else (maybe ten years older than me, not like retirement age). And while he's great in many ways, he apparently CAN. NOT. DEAL. with the minimum requirements of getting lunch together for a dozen or so people. He forgets to get plates. Or to bring napkins. Or he has another meeting right afterward and can't possibly stay to clean up. It's always something, and EVERY SINGLE TIME, a woman—it's always a woman!—will end up running to the kitchen for whatever he forgot or gathering up everyone's trash and food detritus.

It took a while for me to realize this was a full-on pattern, and now I find myself in a blind rage whenever it repeats itself. But I can't figure out how to fix it! The group is usually around 70% women so the "a woman's always the one handling things" thing could be attributed to sheer probability. I don't want to make anyone feel bad—or label myself as a strident feminist killjoy, even though I clearly am one—by making a huge deal about the gender aspect.

But then, you know, he'll come in with pizzas and just set the boxes in the middle of the table while looking around confused as though plates should've magically appeared out of thin air by now, and I can feel hot anger coursing through my entire body.

Can you help me fix this, or at least prevent me from committing murder at our next lunch?

—Feminist SMASH

➡ You know, I've put a lot of effort into ensuring that the advice in this book stays fresh and relevant for years beyond its publication date—but I'd be thrilled if future readers are looking at this section like, "Wait, *sexism?!* How old is this thing??"

And yet sadly I'm not optimistic that what follows will be rendered obsolete anytime soon.

## It's Not Just Sexism, Either

I'm focusing on sexism here because I'm a straight white woman, which means that sexism is the lone -ism of the world that's affected me directly. But this advice can also be useful for victims of racism, homophobia, transphobia, religious intolerance, and whatever other obnoxious exclusionary crap one might encounter in the workplace.

Anything that reduces a human being to a stereotype or set of false assumptions—anything that makes someone feel like they're not afforded the same level of respect as their coworkers for reasons beyond their control—is profoundly Not Okay.

## For All Intents and Purposes

So, let's talk about the breadth of a term like "sexism." On one end of the spectrum you've got some cartoon-level shit: bosses complimenting their female employees' racks and joking (or seriously asserting) that their work performance is subject to the vagaries of hormones. No one in this day and age can pretend that kind of behavior is acceptable in a professional setting, so there's not any plausible deniability for the perpetrator to hide behind. And that, paradoxically, means the most flagrant examples are often the easiest to deal with—or at least, the most straightforward.

Then there's the other kinds of sexism—like the Mystery of Why Only Women Do the Food-Service-y Stuff in this letter. It's *possible* that the dude in that scenario is thinking, "I'm a man, I won't demean myself by procuring plates, that's lady-work"—but more probably, he's not thinking anything beyond, "D'oh, forgot plates again, oh well."

It doesn't matter how innocently a sexist situation arises: it still needs to be corrected once it's brought to light. (The same is true for things like "oh, I didn't realize such-and-such term was a slur"—great, well, now you do, so you can stop using it immediately and apologize to anyone who was within earshot the last time you said it.) Pleading ignorance can be useful in terms of providing context, but it doesn't give anyone license to make the same mistake twice.

### The (Maybe) Accidental Chauvinist

Fortunately—since we can't read minds—the strategy is the same regardless of the thought process behind stuff like this. Unless you're dealing with capital-S, bald-faced sexism, you discuss the problem in neutral terms, leaving the gender aspect out of it as much as possible. It may seem like that's coddling the offending party, but it's not about protecting anyone's feelings— it's about operating from the strongest tactical position.

Think of it this way. If someone *is* harboring prejudicial thoughts, it's unlikely that they're going to reorient their whole worldview after being called out. Whereas if they're just being a doofus, they're likely to get defensive if they're accused of something they don't want to believe about themselves ("I could never be sexist; Ruth Bader Ginsburg is my personal idol; this is madness"). That's not the best response to "check your privilege"–style criticism, but it's a common one, and when it happens it's a distraction.

Your goal is to correct the problem, and someone whose heart was in the right place will probably connect the dots on "oh, I *was* being kinda sexist" without you making that explicit. Plus, the context here is a workplace. With a friend, family member, or partner, you might have a vested interest in educating them, but in an office your priority is just making sure everyone can do their jobs.

### You Don't Have Time for This

Time spent covering for other people's poor planning is time you're not spending on your own work, so focus on that aspect.

For the scenario in the letter, you'd say something like, "Hey Meeting Organizer, can we talk about the setup for these lunches? The past few times we've ended up scrambling around for plates and other supplies, which means we couldn't start on time. That's frustrating for attendees, so can you make sure it's taken care of in the future?" If you want to be a bit more pointed, you can even add ". . . and typically [EXCLUSIVELY FEMALE NAMES] end up handling the place settings, which isn't their job"—but that last part, about "fix this going forward," is key.

### "Woman" Isn't a Job Description

Sometimes the duties of a given position align with certain stereotypes (dudes lifting heavy things, ladies attending to other people's needs, etc.). That can reflect institutionalized sexism too, but it's not really something you can take on until and unless you're involved in hiring new staff members.

Sometimes, though, certain tasks break along gender lines by default—and if that's interfering with your actual work, you're entitled to take action. There's undoubtedly a lot of sociological conditioning at play in these situations, so if you're sitting there thinking "oh my god, why am I always doing the office dishes when I'm a goddamn compliance specialist?" don't feel bad. Maybe you find dish-doing to be therapeutic, even—it's arguably a chance to give your brain a break and feel a sense of accomplishment—and if so I'm not going to say you have to stop because feminism.

The problem arises if you're doing things "because no one else will do them" or because you feel a sense of unspoken obligation—things that have nothing to do with your job description and everything to do with your ladyhood. If there's no one officially responsible for those tasks, then work with your boss to figure out a point person. And if your management team doesn't see the problem, then quietly band together with the other women in your office ("let's all agree that we'll only wash our own dishes from now on," or whatever) until they're forced to acknowledge it.

Every employee deserves to develop their own career without interference, and shouldering other people's burdens definitely qualifies as an impediment.

## Mansplaining by Any Other Name

The other most common form of death-by-a-thousand-cuts sexism is something lately known as "mansplaining"—the maddening phenomenon in which men condescend to women with unnecessary explanations ("Oh, you're a neurosurgeon? Let me tell you all about how the human brain works").

Here I should note that condescension itself knows no gender—a woman can definitely talk down to another woman in an insufferable way, just as a man's explanation to a woman isn't necessarily a mansplanation. That caveat aside, though, there's still a gender bias in the way most people are socialized, which often results in man-people thinking they know better than they actually do. Conversely, woman-people are often taught to be accommodating, which can make it hard for us to feel comfortable saying, "Actually, I've got this [and also, shut up]."

So, let's all try to get more adept at fighting back when we're bombarded with patronizing monologues about our own areas of expertise. It's not always worth the effort—sometimes you'd rather just inwardly roll your eyes at the pomposity of your conversational partner—but if you're dealing with a repeat offender, especially if it's someone you work with regularly, speak up and address it head-on. "Hey, Greg, I know you're trying to be helpful, but it feels kind of condescending when you give me all these 'tips' on stuff I've been handling autonomously for years. Could you knock it off, please?" (The "please" is optional, by the way.)

If you don't want to be quite that direct, just cut things off with "I know! Thanks, can't talk" as soon as the discussion starts heading in that direction. It might feel rude—it might even come across as rude, or at least brusque—but you know what else is rude? Diminishing or outright ignoring someone else's abilities. If your options are "spend each workday quietly seething" or "be slightly snippy to someone who deserves it," I think the choice is pretty clear.

### But What About Flagrant Sexism, Though?

Oh, yeah. Well, sexism of the flat-out flagrant variety starts to bleed into actual harassment, which is just full-on inappropriate—so you can treat it like any other kind of egregiously bad behavior. Phrases like "*Excuse* me?," "I hope you didn't think that was funny," and "I really don't need to hear that kind of thing when I'm trying to work" are all solid comebacks. If the comments persist, you give one final warning about "going to HR," and then follow through on that if your office chauvinist still won't knock it off. All my earlier advice about documentation and major-issue-raising is applicable here too.

If you have the energy—if HR isn't helping or you're incensed enough to enforce some real consequences on your office's resident dirtbag—you can also bring a formal complaint. In the United States, the go-to folks for this are the Equal Employment Opportunity Commission (EEOC), whose jurisdiction typically kicks in once a company has at least fifteen employees (at least as of this writing; check your local listings, especially if you're not based in the USA).

Your options are more limited if you're subjected to varsity-level sexism at a tiny company with no HR department or EEOC oversight. For a job that's otherwise worth keeping (maybe you're paid boatloads of money and your commute is a five-minute walk or something), you can decide to ignore it. Otherwise, you can start planning a speedy exit, and look forward to a lifetime of "your boss said *what?!*" in response to your war stories.

# To Your Health

*Managing medical issues professionally*
*(including but not limited to gestation)*

Dear Businesslady,

I'm starting a new job, and I'm wondering how to handle the fact that I've got a complicated medical situation going on. I look outwardly healthy (whatever "healthy" looks like) but inside I'm kind of a mess. I deal with a smorgasbord of different symptoms, some related to my condition and some that are side effects of medication. Unless I tell the whole sordid story, I get a lot of "oh my cousin had that and cured it with yogurt" or "have you tried [treatment that would honest-to-god kill me]?" But since I need more time off than the average employee (lotsa doctor's appointments, incapacitating flare-ups), being completely secretive isn't really an option.

What's the protocol on mentioning stuff like this to bosses, coworkers, etc.? I don't want to TMI everyone into discomfort, but I also don't want to seem cold and be like "it's a private medical issue" in response to well-meaning questions.

On top of THAT, my boyfriend and I are thinking of starting a family, which is a whole 'nother thing that I'm preemptively worrying about. Even if I could keep my general medical quirkiness to myself, people are going to find out about that soon enough no matter what. So I guess I should just start now? Ugh.

—The Office Sicko

➤ Bodies! You literally can't live without them, and yet our culture tends to get really uncomfortable with even their most straightforward functions. Much as we like to think our brains are running the show, we're all controlled by these weird goopy machines, and sometimes that means our best-laid plans go awry.

A single sick day here or there is one thing. You just send a quick "not feeling well, see you tomorrow" e-mail and that's that. But if you're dealing with a more sustained form of physical upheaval—a chronic health condition, say, or a pregnancy—you're going to have to tell your workplace what's going on.

### First, a PSA

Before I launch into my advice on this stuff, let me say a word about health insurance—or two words, actually: *be covered*. Even if money's tight, even if you're a preternaturally healthy person from a family where everyone dies peacefully in their sleep at 105, even if you're sure you'll get employer-provided coverage in a month or two. At the very least, get some kind of insurance in case of a freak accident or medical emergency. Please.

### Being (a) Patient

If you're dealing with A Medical Issue™, you'll probably have to disclose it to the powers that be at your job. However, the amount of detail or formal documentation that's actually *required* will vary depending on what you need (time off, some kind of special accommodation, etc.), along with state, national, and organizational policies governing your particular situation.

You'll also want to do some soul-searching about how open you want to be, because that's a matter of personal preference. While some conditions still come attached with stigma, discussing them freely might help dispel the notion that Disorder X or Illness Y is some kind of shameful secret. Then again, you're not obligated to serve as the Ambassador for Sufferers of Z to your entire office, so it's really up to you how much you share.

Similarly, you should consider who among your colleagues should be informed. Practically speaking, your boss and HR department (if you have one) are the only people on the need-to-know list, and if you'd like to keep things confidential beyond that, say so. Legally, there are no repercussions if your manager blabs to everyone, so be explicit if you'd like a higher level of discretion. Keep in mind too that it might be useful for your coworkers to have at least a vague understanding of what you're dealing with—if you're going to need a lot of time off, a flexible schedule, or other accommodations, some awareness of your medical escapades might help dispel the notion that you're getting random, unearned preferential treatment.

## A Healthy Amount of Lead Time

Ideally, you'd get your ducks in a row regarding all of these matters before raising your issue with your benefits office—and if we're talking about ongoing or non-urgent conditions, that's the first step. With your homework done, you approach your boss and explain the situation in the most neutral terms possible. Beyond the basics of how this will impact your presence in the office, you can keep the details sparse—but if you'd rather be more candid, that's fine too. Most people will take their cues from you in terms of the emotional register of the conversation, so approaching things with a relatively upbeat tone of "this is the way it is" will probably put you both at ease.

Even if you want to divulge some specifics of what you're dealing with, don't get so graphic that you pull focus away from your professional contributions. Your employer may have certain legal and ethical obligations in terms of how they treat you, but there's no law against getting weirded out, so pull back if you suspect you're veering toward overshare. I *love* talking about medical stuff with a receptive audience, but I've learned that not everyone shares my enthusiasm. Plus, there's a big difference between "I'm trying to figure out why I keep sneezing" and "I've developed a medically anomalous genital rash" in terms of work-appropriate discussion topics. If you're grappling with something on the more private end of the spectrum, there's nothing wrong with saying "I'm having some tests done . . . it's personal" and letting that be that.

## What's the 911?

It gets trickier if you're plunged into the world of healthcare policy without any warning whatsoever. All the previous advice still applies in theory, but you might find yourself in the ER getting prepped for surgery before you realize, oh, I guess I'm gonna be out of the office tomorrow. The next thing you know, you're trying to explain things to your boss through a haze of morphine and pain. Emergency situations are the one time when it's appropriate for someone other than you to communicate with your workplace on your behalf—although even then, you should still be taking the lead to whatever extent you're able.

It's not easy to think about work when you're in a literal life-or-death situation, but unfortunately you can't assume everything will be taken care of without your intervention. Someone—whether it's you, your partner, your friend, a family member, or some combination thereof—needs to be keeping in touch with your office for however long you're away. They need to ask what forms need to be filled out and by whom, provide updates on the timeline of your return (heavily caveated to reflect all the unknowns inherent to medical calamity), and confirm that everything's being documented and processed appropriately by HR or whoever handles such things for your office.

And if whatever's put you out of commission is really serious, that needs to be communicated as well. You don't want to be dealing with mundane, non-urgent job stuff while you're trying to heal.

## Let's Talk About Babies, Baby

Even if you succeed in maintaining a clean bill of health indefinitely, you might still find yourself in need of workplace accommodations due to parenthood. I haven't embarked on that particular life journey myself, but I've consulted several working-mom friends to see what suggestions they had, and their invaluable advice helped inform this section.

Fortunately, babies don't just suddenly appear—whether it's a pregnancy or an adoption, you usually have a fair amount of warning that a child is about to join your household. (Spoiler alert,

I guess, for anyone who still thought they were delivered unexpectedly by storks.) Of course, the actual *moment* of their arrival is often highly unpredictable—"surprise, labor's happening three months early!" or "surprise, the agency found you a kid!"—and in the case of gestation, there are often medical complications beyond the basic bodily strangeness of creating a new human life.

### "FML": It Doesn't Just Stand for "Family Medical Leave"

As soon as parenthood is on your radar, however distantly, start familiarizing yourself with the current iteration of the Family and Medical Leave Act (if you're in the USA) and whatever parental-leave policies exist at your employer.

I'd like to think workplaces will get more parent-friendly as time goes on, but at least right now, the consensus seems to be "parental leave is far shittier than you'd expect it to be." Some places do in fact treat pregnancy/birth like a disability—or at least, construing it as such is the only way to get a good chunk of time off. You might not be able to use your sick days while you're home bonding with your new kid, and/or you might have to burn through all your accrued vacation time. You might not get paid your full salary while you're away, and in some cases you're not even guaranteed to have a job waiting for you when you're past the immediate post-baby phase.

I don't want to stress out would-be parents, but based on my friends' experiences, the whole process is more complicated—and less intuitive—then one might hope. "Fuck My Life," indeed.

### Business as Unusual

Eventually—after some amount of time off spent adjusting to your new arrival—you're going to head back to the office. Or at least I'm supposing as much, based on the topic of this book you're reading.

Some parents take a more extended break from the workforce or opt out entirely, which is also a valid choice. However: even if one parent's salary ends up being entirely devoted to childcare, that doesn't necessarily mean it's "more cost-effective" for that person to stay home with the kid(s). Remaining employed—learning new skills, networking, keeping up with industry trends, and so on—has benefits beyond income alone. Anyone who decides to take a few years off will likely face an uphill climb whenever they try to rejoin the rat race, for whatever that's worth. At the same time, I'm well aware that reputable childcare providers aren't always readily available—which is one of many tough considerations faced by maybe-working parents—and I don't want to suggest that a temporary hiatus from the professional world will make it impossible for you to resume a career down the line.

The transition from "recently be-babied person" back to "employee" might be a bit rocky. Whether you're dying to get back to work after your leave or desperately missing your kid at the office, it's all fine and normal and to be expected. Parenthood is A Big Deal, and so you should cut yourself some slack if you don't seamlessly pivot back to your professional life. Don't let anyone guilt-trip you based on the exact degree you do or don't miss your kid or your job—it's not like there's only one right way to be a good (working) parent. It should get easier over time, and if it doesn't, then you should explore possibilities that might make your life easier: a work-from-home option, a more flexible schedule, or even a different job that's better aligned with your crucial new side gig.

### Nursing: A Grudge

The other "forewarned is forearmed" advice my friends offered concerns nursing. If you're physically producing baby food, then you're going to have to reconcile certain biological realities with the typical prohibition against being topless in the office. (If you don't know what I'm talking about, Google "breast pump" and maybe skip this section until it's more immediately relevant to your life.) Theoretically, you should have at least a few months to figure out a pumping strategy—and start your research sooner rather than later, because workplaces are often woefully underequipped in this regard. You don't want to be relegated to a non-locking conference room, a bathroom (gross, and also illegal by the way, but a sadly common suggestion), or some random pump station that's a twenty-minute walk from your desk.

The ideal setup is a windowless or privacy-screened room with a locking door, and—since you want the ability to work while collecting precious baby-sustenance—it should either be your actual office or equipped with Wi-Fi and a laptop. That might not be feasible (I've heard horror stories about clueless male executives with poor reading comprehension for "do not enter" signs—make sure your chair back is against the door if you're in a room without a lock), but the closer you can get, the better.

### Having It All(ish)

The nursing employee's plight is like a microcosm for working-while-parenting, which is itself not all that different from the issues facing anyone who's professionally employed—whether or not they have kids. You're always dealing with a series of tradeoffs between the ideal, the mediocre, and the unacceptable, and it's up to you to decide whether or not any given situation is good enough. It's just that now you've got to integrate those career decisions with your responsibility for nurturing another human being into adulthood—but don't forget that it's a decades-long process, with plenty of opportunities to make readjustments as you go.

# Bearing Bad News

*How to tell people what they don't want to hear*

Dear Businesslady,

I work at a small liberal arts college where we hire student workers to help with administrative tasks. I'm officially in charge of managing this latest crop of interns—a gift of sorts from my boss because I want to get into "real" management someday and could use the experience.

One student is a great worker, but she's also a budding fashionista and some of her more ambitious looks have been wildly beyond our office's business-casual (but undocumented) dress code. I've been hesitant to bring it up, because I vividly remember how ashamed I felt back in the day when I got chastised about how bare midriffs were verboten on casual Friday. (I hadn't realized there was a gap between my t-shirt and my jeans, and I was mortified.) Plus, I figured her clothing isn't relevant to her otherwise excellent performance.

That was before the provost happened to stop by—afterward, apparently he asked my boss why this student was "dressed for an aerobics class." So I *have* to say something. How can I be firm, but fair, and hopefully not alienate one of our best interns?

—Good Boss, Bad Cop

➡ Feedback may be a gift (see Chapter 3), but it doesn't always feel like that for the recipient. If you're the one *giving* the feedback, it's sometimes the emotional equivalent of giving a six-year-old socks for their birthday: you're trying to be kind, but acutely aware that the recipient is unappreciative of your efforts.

### The Bulletproof Messenger

Yet even though it might kick off a tense discussion, you've got to remain confident when delivering bad news—turning the conversation into a referendum on Feedback, Your Giving Thereof just distracts from the actual issue and prolongs the whole ordeal. You also want to keep things as positive as possible, which is where your tone of voice and demeanor (or the vibe of your e-mail, if you're conveying this in writing) will be key. Your cheerfulness shouldn't seem phony or out-of-sync with the topic at hand, but you want to work against whatever "ugh, I can't do *any*thing right" narrative might be brewing in your audience.

Some people advise the "compliment sandwich" approach, where you nestle your criticism within a couple of positive assessments. That *can* work, but I think it's best limited to scenarios where it's actually sincere—where you really do have a couple of complimentary things to say about whatever you're critiquing. (It also doesn't have to be deployed in a strict "good thing, bad thing, good thing" format either, which feels awkward if you're whiplashing between two unrelated points—plus it's pretty transparent to the many people who are familiar with it as a strategy.)

Instead, whenever you do have some enthusiasm to offer to the conversation, by all means include it. "I think this is an amazing summary of the project" will be a welcome prelude to feedback like "I think we need to tweak the language so it's less jargony," even if the second part is the main thing you want to convey.

### Ripping Off the Band-Aid

Be careful about the ratio of compliments to criticisms, however. If you know (or suspect) that your audience will be unreceptive, you might be reluctant to get to "the bad part"—and that impulse could lead you to nestle your feedback within layers upon layers of protective praise. But going overboard with encouraging comments will dilute your more critical ones to the point of undetectability. You're just wasting their time—and yours—by spinning your wheels because you don't want to hurt someone's feelings.

I guess my point here is: it's okay, sometimes, to hurt people's feelings. That's what feelings are *for*. The person on the receiving end of your suggestions is an adult, and if you cause them to feel bad for a while, they'll get over it eventually.

More importantly, if your message is going to hurt someone's feelings, then there's no avoiding that outcome. You just have to plunge in and get it over with so that you can all move on toward normalcy.

Similarly, resist the urge to couch everything in a series of complex justifications. Even if you're trying to convey "this critique was inevitable," it's not the recipient's job to make you feel better about delivering a tough message. Going on and on—how you wish it weren't so, how the powers that be have forced your hand—just makes the conversation all about you, which isn't appropriate. You shouldn't be bending over backward to protect anyone's feelings, and that includes your own potential discomfort with (temporarily) being disliked.

### Feedback Knows No Hierarchy

While constructive criticism is an essential managerial duty, it doesn't always happen along lines of clear-cut authority. Whenever you're called upon to critique your colleagues' work or point out a problematic aspect of a peer's performance, the attitude is a bit different—more "I'd want to know if it were me," less "I'm telling you what's what." Yet the essentials are the same. Everyone can benefit from an outside perspective on their own work, and people who think otherwise end up shutting down opportunities for their own growth.

In short, if you give some feedback and then get blindsided by an overwhelmingly negative reaction, that doesn't necessarily mean you were out of line. More likely, it means your coworker was more of a fussy baby than you previously realized. And if that happens with someone you manage, then you need to make it clear that such responses aren't acceptable.

### Own Your Own Authority

If you surround your feedback in a cloud of extraneous dialogue, you might introduce the idea that it's up for discussion. In some cases, that's fine—if you and a few other editors are trying to finalize a publication, then a bunch of different opinions might all have their place—but more often you're basically saying "Here's the deal," and you don't want to invite a long, drawn-out argument. The more responsibility you acquire, the more corresponding authority you have to decide when things need to be changed. Delivering periodic criticism is a part of that role, and if you approach it as though it's the most natural thing in the world, the people around you will follow your lead.

# CHAPTER 7

## LIKE A BOSS:

# Making Your Job Work for You

THE EARLY DAYS of your career tend to be focused on "right now," with some vague sense of "later" waiting in the wings. You're eager to acquire some kind of doable job, then develop some semblance of competency at it. While you may have an idea of your next move—the promotions you might pursue, the positions that would be steps up from that initial rung—you know you're not there yet.

I should add, too, that "forging a career" doesn't have to entail an endless series of promotions. There can be many reasons to stay put in any given role, and if you fall into an ideal situation at the beginning of your working life, so much the better. It's like couples who began as high-school sweethearts—sure, those relationships don't *usually* last forever, and yet there are plenty of deeply enamored partners who first started dating in their teens.

Still, for most of us, there are at least a few stages between "first professional job" and "job I want to settle down in." And those intermediate periods can be tricky. You're taking on more responsibilities, but they come with their own stresses and obligations. You're stretching your skills, so you may start making rookie mistakes again right when you were starting to feel like an expert. You're getting restless in your current position, which might mean leaving behind an office that feels like home—or at least, one that's comfortable and familiar. Or you might realize that you've exhausted your ability to grit your teeth and deal with unpleasantness.

As you start preparing for the next-level phase of your career, keep close tabs on your own state of mind. What do you like about your job (the work, the people, the industry), and what don't you like? What would you change if you could? You're in charge of this journey, and while you may not have infinite options available to you, you do have control over the choices you make.

Here's to choosing wisely, and to retiring without regrets.

# Fraud Alert?

## *Dealing with feelings of inadequacy*
## *(A.K.A. Impostor Syndrome)*

Dear Businesslady,

I'm what you'd probably call "successful" by any metric—I'm well paid, I enjoy my work, and I'm surrounded by supportive, like-minded colleagues. My job is challenging enough that I never get bored, and I consistently receive positive feedback from clients.

. . . you're probably wondering "what's the problem?" so here it is: I suffer from impostor syndrome in a major way. Even though I have literal awards in my office attesting to the fact that I know my stuff, I'm constantly convinced that I'm one mistake away from being revealed as an imbecile and a fraud. In my worst, insomniac moments, I compulsively rehearse the apology speech I'd give while being escorted out the door.

I know it's preposterous, but that doesn't change the awful sensation of being unworthy. How can I stop these toxic thoughts?

—Competent by Day, Failure by Night

→ I have a theory about this, which basically boils down to "everyone has impostor syndrome, except people who are the actual worst."

Okay, that's an oversimplification—I don't actually mean to suggest that anyone with a healthy level of self-confidence is somehow deficient. However, I do feel that impostor syndrome—or any related worry-warting about one's own performance—is ultimately the side effect of a desire to do well. That's why it's so common.

The trick is figuring out how to use it to your advantage.

## The Lurking Specter of Inadequacy

Everyone, in every job, starts at the bottom—even superstar employees began with super-basic tasks. As we're learning, we're in a constant state of "try try try FAIL try try try . . ." From the beginning of our careers, we're taught that we're not quite good enough yet, and it can be difficult to break out of that mindset.

Unfortunately, the conventions of the professional world favor criticism over praise. If you mess up, you'll almost certainly hear about it (especially if you're still fairly green), but doing a fantastic job doesn't necessarily garner any special acknowledgment. All of which means that you're probably hearing a disproportionate amount of negative commentary, even if you're actually meeting or exceeding expectations.

So that's one condition that helps provide a breeding ground for impostor syndrome. Another is that we usually don't realize our own mistakes until they're pointed out to us. Sometimes a project you considered finished forever ago will resurface with "needs improvement" metaphorically stamped on it, and then everything else you've done suddenly seems suspect. And who among us hasn't looked back at something we completed months ago, only to discover a glaring typo that no one caught?

Between the preponderance of negative feedback and the (not entirely incorrect) sense that hidden errors lurk everywhere, it's easy to convince yourself that all your accomplishments are secretly worthless. Except—well, except that's not true.

## The Dose Makes the Poison

Left unchecked, impostor syndrome can be debilitating. You can't possibly do your best work while trying to drown out a relentless inner monologue of "you're not good enough and never will be." I've slipped into that kind of poisonous rumination myself, although when it happens I remind myself as quickly as possible that I'm being ridiculous. (I've also noticed it tends to coincide with periods of increased stress, which I'll get into in the next section.)

Yet within the useless negativity of self-doubt there is the kernel of something positive: the idea of infinite potential, of continual improvement.

The only way to get better at anything—any life skill, not just job tasks—is to work at it. You have to exert your best possible effort, look at the results, say "not quite," and then try again. If you have that impulse, it will be the foundation for every success you have in life. It will prompt you to listen attentively when people offer well-meaning critiques, and it will provoke you to find new and better ways to do the things you're good at.

It will also, probably, result in some impostor syndrome. If you see "your personal best" as a constantly moving target, then there's a certain logic to the idea that you could always be working harder. But self-improvement is incremental, and there's nothing wrong with remaining in stasis for a while between big level-up achievements. Let yourself really feel triumphant before you start tackling the next major challenge.

Impostor syndrome is often found palling around with perfectionism, which presents the same kinds of problems. There's a reason we've turned "the perfect is the enemy of the good" into a cliché; I'd also argue that, sometimes, the good is the enemy of the *done*. You're allowed to have high standards, as long as they're not getting in the way of your actual goals.

## I'm #1 So Why Try Harder

So what about those people who don't suffer from impostor syndrome? They're the ones who make a lot of mistakes—more than their fair share, arguably—and yet never seem remotely fazed by it. They send cheerful "I'm a week behind schedule" e-mails that you'd feel ashamed to write, they shrug when you point out glaring inaccuracies, they waltz out of the office at 4 P.M. when everyone else is about to pull an all-nighter.

These people mystify me. How do they just . . . not care? They can be infuriating, too—when you're wracked with self-doubt over some trivial thing you could've done better, their contentment with being borderline incompetent can feel like a personal affront.

I don't know what goes on inside their heads but I've come to realize that their profound chill is a bug, not a feature. It's not something to be envied, even if a certain amount of detachment can be useful in small doses.

### You Earned It

It sucks to work with someone who seems indifferent to their responsibilities, sure. You absolutely don't want to be that person—but if you're scared you might be, then you clearly care too much to fall into that category.

It also sucks to work with someone who's never, ever satisfied. It especially sucks to *be* that person, to remain trapped in a web of pessimism that prevents you from ever feeling a sense of hard-won pride.

It's fine if you check in periodically with your insecurities to see if they have any helpful suggestions to offer. Just remember that they're rarely the voice of reason. Don't let them dominate your interior dialogue—in fact, don't even invite them to partici-pate in the conversation unless you're certain they have something useful to say.

Whatever role you're in, you're there because someone in a position of authority thought you could handle it—and "handling it" doesn't mean "performing flawlessly, never making a single mistake." Trust your management, trust your colleagues, and trust *yourself* that you deserve to be where you are.

And if you can manage to even feel a little bit proud of yourself periodically, then revel in it—you deserve that too.

# Preserving Your Last Nerve

*How to avoid work stress, or at least deal with it*

Dear Businesslady,

I am stressed out pretty much all the time, on a continuum between "active panic attack" and "just really tense." My workload is unusually high for the foreseeable future, and I need to stay in this job for a while because my resume is otherwise full of short stints.

So I make lists and put work blocks on my calendar and do all the right things in terms of staying on top of my priorities. It's not helping. I'm snippy and cranky at the office and snippy and cranky when I get home. I'm not sleeping well and my work/life balance is all out of whack. When I'm working, I'm fixated on how I'm not working fast enough, and when I'm not working, I'm beating myself up about all the stuff that needs to get done.

Feeling like a ball of anxiety all the time is just not sustainable. Am I just not cut out for a demanding job? Even if my current situation improves, I know I'll just find more things to stress about as I take on more and more responsibilities. God, even thinking about it makes me want to burst into tears.

—Why Can't Grown-Ups Have Tantrums?

➤ Tantrum, I feel you. I feel you so hard. Take a long and stress-ful workday, mix in some sleep deprivation and a dash of mis-managed self-care, and even the most hardcore adulting expert will lose their ability to deal. I've been consumed with whiny rage when my 9 P.M. finally-eating-dinner Thai delivery didn't include the chopsticks I specifically requested. And of course, the sense that you're losing a grip on your precious emotional wherewithal isn't exactly encouraging, which in turn leads to meta-stress about feeling so unhinged.

But you *need* that last nerve. You need to be your own shoulder to cry on when it feels like the world is going to shit and no one else is around to comfort you.

### First, Let's Stretch

If Tantrum's plight resonated with you—if you are your-self one botched food order away from unrelenting primal screaming—I want you to put down this book and stretch. Yes, *right now*. If you're in a waiting room or on a train, take a few deep breaths and stretch out your arms and back as subtly as you can while maintaining the social contract. If you're somewhere with more mobility, then go all out, with as much yoga-esque dedica-tion as you can muster. Deep breaths that you take in slowly, hold, and then gradually release. Muscular contortions that make your joints make weird sounds and release tensions you didn't realize you were holding. This isn't about any one specific routine—it's about whatever sequence of movements will make you feel like "man, I just stretched the hell out." (And you subtle, in-public stretchers, do the full version as soon as you can.)

Okay, so, you're back. Don't you feel better? Not "better" as in "fixed" but "better" as in "less bad." I used to pooh-pooh the notion of deliberate stretching protocols (a position perhaps related to the fact that even at my peak personal fitness I can barely touch my toes without bending my knees). But I've been converted.

A good bout of stretching does a few things: it distracts you from whatever you were stressing about, it relaxes the muscular knots that stress causes, and it reminds you that you're a human in a body instead of a brain attached to computer-using hands.

It's easy to say "I can't get up and stretch—every second I have needs to be devoted to finishing this [dumb work thing]." But it's rare to find a project so time sensitive that it prohibits you from spending a couple of minutes being kind to yourself. You'll do better work if you're not seconds from becoming a sobbing wreck.

### Now Go Back in Time and Get More Sleep

Okay, fine, I'm aware of the logistical hurdles to successful time travel. But sleep deprivation makes even the simplest tasks more challenging, and turns complex work stuff into a grueling, torturous slog. Throw some stress-induced insomnia or ill-advised late-in-the-day caffeine into the mix and you'll quickly find yourself locked in a vicious cycle of fatigue and anxiety.

Even though you can't become retroactively well rested, you can resolve to catch as many Zs as possible going forward. Treat yourself to whatever nighttime rituals are the most reliable ways to make you tired, and make a concerted effort to shut off the "work" part of your brain at least an hour before going to bed. Put away your phone if at all possible, or at the very least introduce an embargo on work-related e-mail-checking. If your brain keeps sidling over to job-related stuff, forcibly redirect it to happier, more relaxing, and less worrisome things.

Even if you don't succeed right away, keep at it. Designate bedtime a work-free zone, and then enforce the necessary protocols to keep it that way.

### Inventory (and Liquidation)

Mental disorganization is another hallmark of severe stress. There are legitimate worries (the deadline's tomorrow, need to check in on that project) but they're jumbled together with less pressing concerns (gotta schedule a haircut soon, when am I gonna do laundry) and outright ridiculous ones (I'm gonna get fired, everyone secretly hates me).

So whenever your anxiety is on high alert, do some assessment. Make sure your to-do list is up-to-date so that you can offload some of the taskmaster stuff that's swirling around in your head. Then, think: is anything else bothering you—job-related or otherwise? Being "so stressed about work" can often be a convenient way of repressing other stuff you don't want to deal with, whether it's as major as an unresolved breakup or as minor as your dwindling supply of groceries.

Big emotional issues can—and should—be talked through with your sympathetic ear of choice (friend, therapist, partner, etc.). Your brain isn't great at compartmentalizing, and agita in one aspect of your life will invariably impact unrelated areas. Similarly, you can shut down worries about dumb quotidian tasks *and* treat yourself to a sense of accomplishment by resolving to tackle one chore-type thing every day. Make a list of whatever's on your radar so that you have a roster of semi-therapeutic mini-projects to choose from—you can't de-stress if your personal life is collapsing.

### Maximum Chill

Of course, it's also hard to de-stress while you're running all over town getting coffee with friends and picking up your dry-cleaning. Sometimes you have to commit to chilling the F out, which means treating it with the same level of seriousness that you treat your job. If that seems irresponsible to you, consider this: is it "responsible" to work yourself so ragged that you have a legit mental breakdown, or become too exhausted to operate at full cognitive capacity? (The answer, in case your brain is too overtaxed for rhetorical questions right now, is "No.")

You have to find time in your schedule to recharge, to remind yourself that your personhood exists beyond the boundaries of your office. To seek out and indulge in the things that bring you joy. If you have to leave work early or even call in sick, then do it—not, like, *all the time*, obviously, but if that's the only way to carve out some space in your schedule for revitalization, then so be it. When you're feeling completely overwhelmed by stress, it's a "by any means necessary" situation.

Engaging in dedicated self-care isn't selfish, and the more you insist "I'm far too busy for that" the more necessary it probably is. Your brain, like any machine, can't function at top speed indefinitely. Often, you'll find yourself getting unstuck on whatever problems were bothering you after a period of concerted downtime. And regardless, a more relaxed, refreshed, and well-rested you will be a better colleague and professional contributor. If you can't do it for yourself, consider it an obligatory gift to your coworkers.

# Let Me Get That for You

*Expanding your role, even if it's a stretch*

Dear Businesslady,

I'm in the career-path equivalent of staring wistfully out a classroom window on a gorgeous sunny day.

I'd love to stick with my company long-term, and there are a lot of higher-ranking jobs I think I'd be good at—either right now or after I get a bit more experience. For the time being, though, I'm relegated to an entry-level position with rigidly defined duties that I'm starting to get tired of.

I've talked to my boss about my interest in growing my skillset, and he's supportive in theory, but no one senior to me has the time for mentorship or including me in new projects. But then when I ask about a possible promotion, everyone points out that I haven't proven myself at such-and-such task yet—even though I'm desperate for the chance to learn!

Should I start stalking the people in the jobs I covet so I can learn their secrets, or just accept that I'll need to switch companies if I want to grow?

—Put Me In, Coach!

➤ This is one of the most frustrating paradoxes of the early-career period: you want to gain experience, yet you're too inexperienced to be involved in areas where you could acquire it.

Your senior coworkers aren't just being obstructionists, either. It's a lot more work to train someone on a task than to do it—so if they don't actually *have* to show you the ropes, they have a strong incentive to maintain the status quo. After all, everyone's busy.

The only way past this impasse is to somehow justify their efforts and make it worth their while. But first, let your boss in on your plans.

### Unauthorized Extracurriculars

That's right, you should apprise your boss of your intentions before you start cozying up to well-placed coworkers. I mean, it's fine if you say "hi" to them a few times, but you shouldn't start inserting yourself into new projects without your manager's blessing.

It seems unfair that you could be told "no, I refuse to let you develop your skills," but such are the strictures of an office structure. Your boss might have all kinds of reasons to keep you focused on your official duties—maybe the department you're interested in working with is about to be massively reorganized, maybe your would-be mentor is actually terrible at their job, maybe they're afraid you'll jump ship as soon as you've gotten a glimpse of the world beyond your current role. Or maybe you're still not quite up to speed yet and they're concerned about how your performance might suffer with even more on your plate.

Whatever their rationale, your boss is in fact the boss of you, so you have to let them decide whether you're allowed to start branching out. However, hearing "no" once doesn't mean you're banned from asking forever. You can't keep raising the issue with such regularity that you become a pest, but you can revisit it at intervals—especially during performance evaluations (more on those in the next section) and other big-picture conversations about your professional future.

## Part of Your World

The longer you've been in the same role, the likelier it is that your manager will support some expansion in your duties and experience. Unless your office culture is one where internal promotions are exceedingly rare, or your job is completely disconnected from the work of any senior colleagues, it's ultimately in the organization's best interest to allow you to develop your skills—they presumably want their good employees to stick around, and there are obvious advantages to having a well-rounded staff.

Especially once you're a year or two out from your hire date, it's reasonable to get more emphatic about your desire for growth. You don't have to actually say the words "or else I'll start job-searching" because any mention of dissatisfaction and boredom will send that message to all but the most obtuse of managers. (And if you still get nowhere, you can make good on that implicit threat—even if you haven't added huge new abilities to your skillset, you're still going to be a more attractive candidate than you used to be.)

Ideally, though, your boss will be an ally in setting you up with a potential mentor, which can be crucial if you haven't been able to make those connections on your own. There's a big difference between an underling asking to be included on something and a peer (or superior) explicitly saying, "We'd like Chelsea to learn more about HR, so please find ways to involve her in your operations."

## Right Here Waiting

Infiltrating the world of the higher-ups isn't something that happens all at once. Instead, you need to start small—figure out which colleagues are the gatekeepers to the temple of advanced knowledge you seek, and make yourself known to them. If they're in an office chitchat circle, stop by and join in. If your job overlaps with theirs, even slightly, try to identify ways you can make their life easier. Once you've established a rapport—when you've become That Nice Kid from Marketing instead of an unfamiliar newbie—pop the question. "You know, I'd love to gain some experience in [your field]. Are there any projects I could pitch in on?"

Chances are the answer will be "no" at first, but at least your interest is out there. As time goes on, continue checking in periodically, especially if you notice a particular opportunity (e.g., "My team puts together blurbs that are a lot like the ones you use for reports. Could I do some first drafts for you? It would be great practice for me, and I'm sure I'd learn a lot from your edits").

Whatever angle you're working, try to focus on the skills you *do* have to offer, along with your eagerness to benefit from their wisdom. You're more likely to strike out if your requests for increased involvement coincide with particularly busy times, so plan accordingly.

It will probably take a while before you're actually given your shot, but that's fine—after all, you still have the rest of your job to do, and you won't get promoted if you let that lapse during your quest.

### Not Throwing Away Your Shot

The eventual reward for all this stalking around and insinuating yourself into higher-level work is, obviously, a higher-ranking role. But until you reach the point where you're ready to officially level up, you have to make sure you're not focused on the future at the expense of the present.

While tackling stretch projects and planning for your next move is commendable, ignoring your responsibilities in favor of shiny new skills is . . . the opposite of that. You're not going to impress anyone by jumping the gun—least of all your peers, who will end up picking up your slack if you try to abandon them prematurely. And managers will be extremely reluctant to promote (or give a good reference for) someone whose self-interest is stronger than their work ethic.

So, keep your aspirations high but keep your perspective realistic. Until you get that fancy new job, stay in your lane with all the patience you can muster.

# Moving On Up

*Championing your own achievements and getting recognition (raises, promotions, etc.)*

Dear Businesslady,

I need help getting over my uneasiness with self-promotion. I've been at the same organization for a few years, and I've taken on more and more responsibility. Each time, though, it's sort of been because something has fallen in my lap—like a job opened up one level above me right as I happened to help the hiring manager with a special project, and thus I got a promotion.

Now, I'm an "acting" client manager at one level above my official title, simply because the person I'd been assisting quit abruptly and I was the logical person to step in. But even though I'm doing the work of a more senior person, my title—and, to be all gross and mercenary, my pay—are still at the lower rank.

Literally everyone who's heard me explain this situation is like, "ASK THEM FOR MORE MONEY" but . . . that's a hard conversation to have! I don't want to make things uncomfortable if they turn me down, and I especially don't want to seem unappreciative of all the opportunities they've given me. I guess I'm just kind of hoping another position will open up, so I can apply through formal channels and never have to have The Talk . . . although I guess I won't be able to ride to retirement on a series of effortless promotions.

—Reluctant Tooter of My Own Horn

➤ It can be awkward and uncomfortable to say nice things about yourself. Culturally, a lot of people are brought up believing that it's inappropriate, unseemly, or at least impolite. Which, sure—socially speaking, you need to be judicious about how many stories you tell about The Greatness of You, or else no one's going to be super-psyched to be in your vicinity.

That's the best thing about working for a living, though: it's the one opportunity you have in life to be shamelessly* self-promoting without needing to apologize for it.

*Not "shamelessly" in the sense of "abandoning all moral principles for the sake of your own personal gain," but in the sense of refusing to feel guilty about the fact that you're pleased with your own accomplishments.

### You Don't Save Me, I Save Me

Don't forget: no one will ever tell you that you're working too hard. Similarly, it's extraordinarily rare for management to pull you aside, give you a fist bump, and say, "You just got yourself a raise." Even if you leave aside the obvious ridiculousness of that exact scenario, it's still not a common occurrence in the abstract, either.

My point is, promotions don't happen *to* you nearly as often as you *make* them happen. The inertia of an office dynamic is a powerful thing, and that discourages the powers that be from making any drastic moves. Even if you're arguably "too good" for a particular position, it benefits your organization to have someone performing at above-and-beyond levels. They lucked out and now have the most talented [that role] imaginable—why would they go out of their way to change that?

Most of the time, in order to get meaningfully rewarded for your work, you have to ask. If you're happy with how things are, then there's no reason to request more—but if you'd like some extra recognition, you're going to have to be your own self-advocate.

### Perform, and Be Evaluated

It's here that I'd like to pause and discuss performance evaluations, because I think this is the context in which they should be considered. True, annual assessments are not the most fun thing ever—they're time-consuming and can be weirdly intimate and involve the kind of forthright discussion that most social rules are designed to avoid.

They're also essential, though, for giving bosses and employees the chance to discuss how things are going. So much of working life is about patterns, and performance evaluations are an opportunity to say "here are the patterns I'm seeing"—for managers as well as the people they manage.

It's natural to feel nervous going into an assessment, especially if your supervisor tends to be hands-off or if you know you're probably going to get dinged for some recent mistakes. For those who are having trouble fighting off the scourge of impostor syndrome, that'll be flaring up too. But the best way to quell those anxieties is by arming yourself with cold, hard facts about what a rockstar you are.

Performance evaluations are the perfect excuse to say, "Hey, check out the awesome job I've been doing." If you've gotten compliments that seemed too insubstantial to mention individually, aggregate them to reflect the overall trend of people appreciating your work. If you've met or exceeded quantifiable benchmarks—whether in terms of official goals or your own independent tracking—make sure that's known.

Your evaluation might include some tough feedback, but at least you'll be able to point out what you've accomplished in your better moments. (Plus, even the most brutal performance evaluation comes equipped with a shot at redemption. Once you know what you're doing wrong, you can fix it, and it's easier to end things on a positive note if you've got a dossier attesting to how hard you work.)

And if everything goes better than expected, you'll be able to keep the momentum going by adding your own observations about everything you've achieved. It's an unequivocal win/win.

### Look on My Works, Ye Bosses, and . . . Be Impressed

If you read Chapter 3, you're already keeping a file of the positive feedback you've received. Here's where that archive becomes incredibly valuable.

At every opportunity for championing your work accomplishments (whether it's a performance evaluation or otherwise), sit down and think of everything you've done in the recent past. After you've gotten your list together, go through your compliment file and see if it jogs your memory about anything else—it probably will, and if nothing else you can back up key achievements with especially effusive endorsements.

Sometimes you'll be asked to provide a self-assessment, in which case this stuff is the perfect fodder. And if your own input isn't directly requested, you can still compile the most significant items from your master list into a document you carry with you at important State of Your Job–type meetings. It's maddening when you leave a conversation and then retroactively think of something you definitely should've mentioned, and this cheat sheet will prevent that frustration.

### You Can Sometimes Get What You Want

Whenever you're having a big-time assessment talk, it's a negotiation of sorts, and it's always best to enter a negotiation with a decently well-formed sense of what you want. Before the conversation begins, think about your ideal outcome—whether it's a fancier title, additional pay, different responsibilities, or a new job altogether—and weigh that against what you know about your organization. There may be times where it makes strategic sense to ask for something unprecedented and extreme, but you want to be prepared for the reaction that's likely to generate.

Even though performance evaluations are the most readily available opportunities for having these kinds of discussions, they're not the only way to make them happen. Knowing what you want includes knowing "I want to talk about my job situation" and then asking for a chunk of your manager's time. As with any major meeting, you may have to wait a bit until the timing's right, but any halfway competent boss will be willing to hear you out eventually.

## Say It Right

The actual speaking-aloud part of this operation is quite possibly the hardest part. You can't just throw down your armful of printed-out e-mail accolades and then run out of your manager's office—or, I mean, you can, but it's probably not going to get the results you were hoping for.

Nope, you're going to have to actually use your mouth to say complimentary things about your very own self. I promise, you can handle it.

As always, a matter-of-fact tone is your life raft for delicate conversational situations. When you explain how well you've been doing, you're simply conveying the facts—nothing weird about that!

As you run through your talking points, it'll probably feel more natural if you use phrases like "I'm really proud of," "A lot of people were happy about," and "I was really pleased that." In other words, put the emphasis on how good *you* feel about doing good work for the company. Even if you actually hate your job (that happens, and it's next on the list of topics), surely you get some joy in doing it well, right? Or at least you're glad that it's not a constant struggle? Whatever your perspective, just focus on some believable version of "seriously, I'm pretty great at this."

## Can You Meet Me Halfway?

Here's where I regret to inform you that no iteration of "seriously, I'm pretty great at this" works as a magic spell to unlock raises and promotions. You may even be lucky enough to get everything you've asked for, but it won't happen immediately. Few bosses have the authority to change titles or increase salaries on the spot, and the ones who do tend to give it some consideration. As long as you get an encouraging response, try to be patient and see where things go from there.

It's also totally possible that you'll get a less enthusiastic reaction, in which case you'll have to make some compromises. Express appropriately tempered disappointment, and suggest some alternate option that splits the difference between your respective positions. Often the impasse will have to do with available funding (i.e., you want more money that they don't have), so take note of the fact that some perks—new titles, more flexible schedules, adjusted duties—don't necessarily come with a price tag.

### (Just Like) Starting Over

At the end of this arduous exercise in self-promotion will be the result: victory, defeat, or something in between. If it's victory, well, yay! Enjoy your hard-earned success and accept any and all congratulations that come your way. Achievement unlocked: You've entered the next phase of your career.

In scenarios of less clear-cut triumph, you have one of two options: stick it out for a while, or start looking elsewhere. If you decide to stay put, then try to find ways to be happy about it—or at least, not actively disgruntled. (It's possible, I swear—keep reading.) And if you decide to move on, then all of the aforementioned discussion of your own achievements will be great practice for the job interviews that are about to appear in your immediate future.

# This Isn't Working

*A survival guide for the burnt-out and stuck*

Dear Businesslady,

I am beyond ready to quit my job. Forget yesterday—I wish I could quit my job effective eight months ago, which is when I started job-searching. But I can't find anything. Or at least, I can't find anything worth leaving this job over, even though I'm becoming more desperate with every passing day.

In the meantime, I'm just becoming a worse and worse employee, and it's starting to get depressing. I'm bored and I'm irritated beyond belief with petty office politics. Each morning I fantasize about calling in sick (and then actually do call in sick if I think it's been long enough since I last played hooky).

Someone's eventually gonna notice how checked out I am and I'm sure there will be consequences, but worrying about that doesn't help—it just makes me angrier that I haven't managed to escape. Should I just flip everyone the bird one day, walk out, and then live off my savings until something better finally comes along?

—One More Day Is Too Many

So, a fact of the working world is that people leave jobs. Sometimes you leave regretfully—because you're moving away, because you're getting laid off, or simply because you stumbled into an even better job you couldn't pass up.

Other times, you leave like you're running out of a burning building full of zombies.

Until you're ready to escape, though, it's best if you don't treat your coworkers like monsters or avoid your office as though it were a structure fire. Even jobs that have become intolerable are a part of your professional profile, and you can do lasting damage to your reputation by blowing them off in the eleventh hour.

### Let's Not Make It Harder Than It Has to Be

You'll know when you've reached your breaking point with a job—and ideally, you'll find a way to extricate yourself before that happens. But sometimes you don't have control over the timing of your exit, and for whatever reason, you find yourself trapped in a position that has lost its luster.

When you're stuck like this, you can spin yourself into a wholly negative headspace with surprising speed. If you look at the world around you through the lens of "this sucks," you'll be hypersensitive to anything that confirms your perspective. Work is already an obligation and an imposition on your personal time—feeling like it's also *excruciating* can really wear on you. And if your listlessness metastasizes into decreased effort, then the cycle accelerates even faster. Unless you're a total genius at your job and/or have the easiest position ever, checking out is going to make your job even more annoying because you're constantly dealing with the consequences of your own shoddy work.

This is a really dangerous spot to be in, careerwise. If it's limited to the short senioritis period before you leave one job for another one, then you might be able to get away with it—coworkers may not notice that you have one foot out the door, or they may forgive it in light of your previous history. It's a real problem, though, if you transform into the office sourpuss for an indefinite period of time. Colleagues will eventually stop judging you based on the employee you used to be, at which point they're unlikely to help you launch into a new position.

## What's the Angle Here?

As long as you're imprisoned in the Worst Job Ever, you might as well get something out of it. For starters, you're already getting a salary—so you've got that going for you, which is nice.

There are also probably learning opportunities somewhere within the hellscape that is your workplace, so distract yourself from how much you hate your job by figuring out what those might be. You can try to pick up some new skills, for instance—no one has to know that you have the ulterior motive of building the ladder that you'll use to climb to freedom. Especially if you're striking out in an interminable job search, finding a way to beef up your resume is a great way to kill time while you're in professional purgatory.

You might be sick of your job because it's a nightmarish place to work—bad management, worse business practices. If you feel sufficiently motivated, why not see if it's possible to make some kind of positive improvement in the culture? Don't go on a hopeless crusade or alienate all the managers you'll need as references someday, but feel free to push back a little at all the inanity around you. Sometimes that "out of fucks to give" position is a great opportunity to see how assertive you're able to be, or how much you can get people to listen to you if you're willing to make an impassioned point.

If nothing else, your office should give you some clear negative boundaries that you can use to inform your future career decisions: what you don't like, what drives you crazy, what you can look for as red flags signaling dysfunction. Basically, a shitty job is like boot camp—because it's difficult and unpleasant, it'll make you stronger in the long run.

## Dig Your Way Out

By the way, when I talk about people who are "stuck" in a job, I'm assuming there's some reason they can't leave or else that they haven't been able to land a new position yet. If you feel even the slightest hint of contempt brewing for your workplace, that means it's time to make a new run at the job market.

Don't forget that getting hired can take approximately forever—you don't want to become entirely frustrated with your current position before you've managed to find a new one. Also, you're never obligated to take any job you're offered. Sometimes, seeing inside another office and meeting a different manager are great ways to gain much-needed perspective on your own situation.

Even if they don't end in offers, applications and interviews can be powerful experiences. They allow you to reconsider your skills and experience beyond the office where you developed them, and imagine new possibilities.

Speaking of your resume, it's been a while since you wrote that thing, right? Now that you've got a whole file of badass accomplishments, start adding them in. Take a moment to admire how much more you've done, and get psyched about all the jobs you've become qualified for. Once you see a position you want to pursue, redo your cover letter too. Tell a new story about the professional you've become, and all the capabilities you can offer a worthy organization.

### This Too Shall Pass

Even if it *seems* like a prison, you will eventually get to leave your job. Soon, your whole world will shift, and before you know it your old office will fade into distant memory. The things that infuriated you will just seem silly, and the worst parts will become well-worn anecdotes you deploy for laughs and commiseration. Don't waste your energy holding a grudge against an old job, no matter how legitimately terrible it may've been—it was a chapter in your life that's now over, and somehow it helped get you to wherever you ended up.

# File under "Pastures, Greener"

*Quitting your job guilt-free and leaving on good terms*

Dear Businesslady,

For the past year and a half I've been the office manager of a small company: I track absences, schedule meetings, keep us stocked with supplies, and manage most of our correspondence with clients. I also organize birthday celebrations and stay on top of other "extra" things to keep the workplace a nice place to be. Everyone is constantly praising my work ethic and talking about how I'm "the person holding this place together."

Here's the thing: I think this job has run its course. I spend 75% of my day bored out of my mind, and the other 25% stressed out over the latest mini-crisis. There's no opportunity for advancement at this company—they manufacture a niche product, and they don't do marketing so there's no possibility of incorporating that into my role. I majored in communications in college and would love to do something with social media or some of the other things I studied, but I think I'll have to move on in order to make that happen.

I'm afraid of leaving this community where I'm truly valued, I'm worried about how they'll manage without me, and I feel guilty. The last time I mentioned my frustrations to the owner, he said he'd pay me anything I asked for in order to keep me—but I don't want more money, I want a new job! Except that feels incredibly selfish, and I'm also a little scared about whether I'll actually be able to work my way up in a new field.

Help!

—Ungrateful Flight Risk

➡ Well-paid people never want to leave their jobs, right? Wrong. No matter how big, your paycheck still won't prevent you from feeling stifled by the knowledge that you won't ever advance in your company. It's natural to yearn for new challenges, especially after a few years of doing the same thing.

If you're in this spot, you probably already know what you need to do: find a better job, and then leave your current one. So you need to get comfortable enough with that idea to actually do it. If you hesitate, you might find your vague sense of dissatisfaction curdling into active resentment, with all the unpleasantness that entails.

## Make Me a Match

Of all the ways in which job-searching is like dating (even as they're blessedly very different), one of the similarities is how your perspective shifts as you begin to understand the options available to you. Early in your romantic life, the very idea that *anyone* might be interested in you is enthralling. As long as there's some degree of reciprocity on your end, that's usually enough to make you start doodling hearts on the nearest available blank surface.

But then you get older, get a bit more experience under your belt, and eventually start saying things like "so-and-so is a great person but the feeling just isn't mutual." By the time you're an independent adult, the idea of pursuing a romantic relationship on the sole grounds of "someone else is attracted to you" (with an implied "and what are the odds of *that* ever happening again?") doesn't meet the bar for being a good idea.

Similarly, most careers begin with a fairly desperate need for gainful employment with few considerations beyond that. But once the novelty of simply having a job wears off—and especially if you've outgrown your current position—you'll start getting antsy for a better fit.

## The [Something]-Year Itch

So, take a deep breath and admit that you, like countless others, want to leave your job for a different one. The exact reasons don't matter, even if they're as hazy as "kinda wanna see what it's like." It might feel strange if you've never known anything else (and can be especially jarring if you're working for a small, tight-knit company), but moving on is a standard element of the professional lifecycle. It doesn't make you a bad person or an ungrateful one, and it doesn't mean you'll be sabotaging your workplace on your way out the door. It's not uncommon for comments about indispensability to circulate in the airspace of especially competent people, and hard workers can have a very real impact on day-to-day operations. But remember: you got trained into your current role by someone, and in many cases that person was in the position even longer than you. Logic suggests that your organization will eventually find a new employee who can keep things running just as smoothly.

That means you need to begin job-searching (and for a refresher on that, see Chapter 1). Talk to your friends with backgrounds similar to yours who seem really happy in their jobs, and see if there are openings where they work. Begin reading postings to see what appeals to you. Get your resume up-to-date so that it reflects all you've accomplished since you were last on the market. Even if you want your next role to shift more toward your field (the marketing/social-media-guru side of things in the previous example, or whatever area of the working world most appeals to you), you can find a way to spin all your recent responsibilities as evidence of your professional skills: juggling multiple priorities, time management, customer service, organization, and so on—adjusted for your actual experience and the position you're gunning for.

### Breaking Up

Depending on your relationship with your boss, you might want to be up-front about your plans even before you've started sending out applications. You might also worry that they won't take it well, in which case you're fully within your rights to keep mum until you have an offer in hand. Either way, when it's time to have the "I'm leaving" talk, you can assuage any feelings of guilt by giving plenty of notice, providing meticulous documentation on your various ongoing tasks, and—if time allows—offering your assistance in hiring and/or training your replacement.

You might feel conflicted as you actually prepare to move on, and that's normal too. If possible, try to prepare yourself for the onslaught of complicated emotions by finding things to appreciate about your current job while you're still there. If you think of it as a temporary stop on your overall career journey—as opposed to the place where you're trapped forever due to your irreplaceability—you'll get more enjoyment out of your remaining tenure.

### Resigning Yourself

It's worth noting that even though a "resignation letter" is a thing you hear about, you probably won't provide written documentation as the first step in your departure. Sometimes there will be official paperwork concerning your last day and final paycheck, but that usually appears after your boss has already learned that you're heading off into the sunset. So after you've accepted a job offer—or after you've got enough money in savings to cushion you through a jobless period of indeterminate length—schedule a conversation with your manager in which you break the news. There may be tears (yours, theirs, both), or it may be as seamless as them saying, "Yeah, I figured that was on the horizon; best of luck." One way or another, it will end with a mutually agreed-upon last day and a preliminary discussion of transition logistics. You should plan on giving your old job at least two weeks of your time before heading out—more if you're in a busy season or on the cusp of some big project you're an integral part of—but in some situations your boss might be like, "cool, your last day is now," so if that happens, don't panic. Your new job might be able to move up your start date in response to an accelerated departure, but even if they can't or won't, you're now in the not-actually-terrible position of having some extra downtime.

### Brave New World

Whenever you do make your move, you'll have to readjust to a whole new workplace, but keep in mind: you've already proven you can hack it in a professional context, so the odds of outright failure are really low. Plus, your previous experience will make you a much more attractive candidate than someone straight out of college even if you haven't done anything in your desired field just yet. You may not find your forever job right away, but as long as you feel like you're headed in the right direction, that's all that matters.

### So Long, Farewell

If all goes according to plan, your current coworkers will handle the news of your departure amiably, thanking you for all your hard work and sending you on your way with only a minimum of guilt-tripping—most of it, hopefully, inadvertent. Although, alas, not everyone is capable of basic courtesy. If you start getting a vibe of "how could you" after you've given notice, just keep your head held high and take comfort in the fact that a few years from now, you'll be remembered as a valuable employee and not as the architect of an unspeakable betrayal.

### A Graceful (and Gracious) Exit

Your career should take you to roles and jobs that work best for *you*. It's great if that aligns with the best interest of whatever organization you work for, but sometimes your paths diverge, and that's to be expected—you shouldn't expect backlash in response to a job change. As long as you give plenty of notice, and assist (within reason) with the transition, you should expect support from your coworkers and your soon-to-be-former boss as you set off for greener pastures. Thank everyone you worked with and make plans to keep in touch with the people you were closest to—you never know how and when they might reappear in your professional future, or whether they might help you snag another new job someday.

Go ahead and cut that tie completely once you're out the door, though. Beyond the first week, no one should be asking you where things are or trying to coax you into continuing your old job as an unpaid internship. For bonus points, and if you can afford it, go ahead and schedule your start date with the new gig a week or so out from your last day at your old job—the feeling of *not being in charge of anything* is more delicious than any vacation, especially when there's no nagging worry about unemployment to take away from it.

# I Guess This Is Working, Then

## A Job You Don't Hate and a Life You Enjoy

Yep, welcome to the lifestyle of the gainfully employed. From now on, it's just an ongoing calculus of salary, workload, environment, responsibilities, fit, and whatever other factors matter to you in terms of how you spend your weekdays.

The end goal is ending up in a professional situation that feels comfortable to *you* (regardless of how it aligns with anyone else's standards or expectations). In the meantime—while you're in all those less-than-ideal jobs that will pave your path to success—you should be improving yourself in the hope of moving forward. Every office has something instructive to offer, even if (in the worst-case scenario) it's "FYI, you hate this." Keep your eyes and mind open, and you'll be able to continually pick up new skills and tidbits of expertise that you can use to propel yourself into the next promising opportunity.

That's working. That's a career. That's how you write yourself into your own life story.

# The Book Ends but
# the Conversation Doesn't

IF YOU GET stuck along the way—or if you're struggling with a situation that I've somehow failed to cover—rest assured that Businesslady's still got your back. You can hit me up on Twitter (@YrBusinesslady), follow me on Facebook (@DearBusinesslady) and Medium (@YrBusinesslady), or e-mail me for advice tailored specifically to you (DearBusinesslady@gmail.com). I'd love to hear from my readers!

Now go forth and work your magic.

# Acknowledgments

This book is a reflection of all the experiences I've accrued in my professional life and beyond, which means it's hugely indebted to a host of other people. I want to express my gratitude to anyone who's ever inspired, edited, or encouraged me, with particular thanks to:

All my previous managers and bosses, each of whom supported and challenged me in influential ways—especially Katie Malmquist, Simrit Dhesi, and Martha T. Roth (whose editorial critiques offered the best writerly training I could've ever hoped for).

The many coworkers who have become friends—too many to name, but each of whom I'm tremendously lucky to have in my life. You know who you are, and you know that you made life livable during the most stressful times.

My castmates, collaborators, and trainers in the Off-Off Campus comedy troupe at the University of Chicago. You taught me how to be funny, and how to develop creative material in consultation with other people—which means that arguably you're the reason this book exists.

My fabulous friends (the few I didn't meet through work or OOC). You guys are fantastic and my life is better for having known you. Special thanks go out to Shuka Moshiri and Tatyana Telnikova for a half-lifetime's worth of love and awesomeness.

The various editors who helped me find my voice and hone it for different audiences. I'm particularly grateful to the folks who brought the Dear Businesslady column into being—Nicole Chung, Nicole Cliffe, and Mallory Ortberg of The Toast (RIP)—as well as Ester Bloom, Nicole Dieker, and Megan Reynolds of The Billfold for keeping it going.

Every educator who was responsible for shaping my worldview: my preschool through sixth-grade teachers, the faculty of

John Burroughs School, my professors and lecturers in the College at the University of Chicago, and most recently my instructors in the Editing certificate program at the UChicago Graham School.

A whole Internet's worth of fellow advice columnists, for their enlightenment and inspiration. On that note, anyone who's not already reading Ask a Manager or Captain Awkward needs to go bask in their wisdom immediately.

The good people of Adams Media who allowed me to fulfill a lifelong dream of becoming a published author—notably Becky Tarr Thomas and Laura Daly, my intrepid guides throughout the writing process.

The working moms who helped with Chapter 6: Analiese Wilcox Marchesseault, Erin Will Midtlyng, Sally Bell Pierce (who deserves additional recognition for nearly three decades of friendship), Becky Popelka, and Miranda Swanson.

The dozens of semi-anonymous and often faceless people online—on Tumblr, in the comment threads of *The Hairpin* and *The Toast*, and elsewhere—who helped me feel confident in sharing my opinions with the world.

Everyone else who had a hand in this book's creation, including but not limited to Leila Sales (an OOC alum, an extremely talented young-adult novelist, and an all-around excellent human being). She demystified the publishing industry for me, and her agent, Stephen Barbara, was kind enough to be generous with his expertise as I considered this new endeavor.

My amazing family—both the one I was born into and the one I was fortunate enough to join via marriage. Extra bonus thanks to my parents, Loren and Rhonda Wassell, for ensuring I'd grow up proficient in the ways of the written word—and for indulging my youthful forays into monkeyland.

Finally, nothing in my life would be the same without my husband, Doug Guerra, an incomparable friend, partner, confidant, interlocutor, castmate, editor, collaborator, competitor, companion, tactical buddy, and big boss.

. . . I'm not crying, *you're* crying. Thank you, thank you, thank you.

# Index